What People Are Saying About
Secrets of the Millionaire Inside

"There are many books out there that claim to provide you with the secret key to wealth and happiness and but few deliver, until now. *Secrets of the Millionaire Inside* is like the gift that keeps giving. Paul McCormick has delivered an approach that will change your life for good. Unlike the many books out there, *Secrets* delivers and invites you to step into the world of unlimited possibilities every day. *Secrets* is about empowerment, knowledge, and manifestation. Get ready to receive unlimited wealth and abundance now."

~ Dr. Pat Baccili
The Dr. Pat Show – Talk Radio to Thrive By
www.thedrpatshow.com

"I love this book! It's not just about how to create massive amounts of wealth, but also about discovering the secrets to proactively creating whatever it is you want in life – freedom, peace, happiness, and more. I'd recommend it to anyone."

~ "Dr. Proactive" Randy Gilbert,
founder of InsideSuccessNetwork.com

"This book is not just about how to create massive amounts of wealth. It's about encouraging you to think without limits, to believe in yourself, to imagine the possibilities, to stop fearing and to make your life whatever you want it to be."

~ DC Cordova, CEO,
Excellerated Business Schools®/Money & You® Program
www.excellerated.com

"Paul's book shows the outward process of building wealth while at the same time shows the inner journey of thinking from a place of abundance, freedom, and joy. If you want to discover how to be happy on the inside and incredibly wealthy on the outside then read this book."

~ Peggy McColl, New York Times Best-Selling Author of
Your Destiny Switch

"Paul McCormick's book, *Secrets of the Millionaire Inside,* shows not only how to develop financial freedom, but also shows how to change your thoughts and actions to create the life you've always dreamed of having. By implementing the techniques outlined in this book, you are taking the purposeful, proven steps that lead to a life of fulfillment and wealth."

~ Ivan Misner, NY Times *bestselling author and founder of BNI*

"If you want to know how ordinary people become extraordinary then read this book. It shows in an easy step by step process how to change your thoughts and actions to create the positive life you desire and how to have it all – financial freedom and happiness all at the same time. It reveals how it is possible for everyday people to create their own miracles… every day."

~ Amy "AJ" Crowell, author of Loved Back to Life

"Whether you work for minimum wage or are a wealthy CEO, *Secrets of the Millionaire Inside* challenges you to push your limits to become wealthy and free beyond limit. This is the formula for success that all of the greatest people throughout history have used to achieve greatness. It's all here in this simple to follow 7-step formula."

~ John Carpenter Dealey, philanthropist, author, founder of MasterMindSoaring.com

"Finally, a book about true wealth that focuses not just on how to make money, but changes how you think about everything. This book will transform you, help you to Step Up and win more, and bring financial freedom to your life and business."

~ Daniel Grissom, CEO, PhDinResults, and national bestselling author of Step Up!

"When I first saw Paul's book I thought, 'Oh no, another book about how to make money...' Wrong! *Secrets of the Millionaire Inside* is about much more than money. It's about abundance, riches, wealth, and happiness – inside and out. There are some brilliant insights in this book, presented in ways that grabbed my attention. I saw some simple little twists and changes I can make in my thinking and actions that have already begun producing good results, much easier than my previous approaches. Many have said, 'Do what you love and love what you do,' and 'Do what you love and the money will follow.' Paul shows us the formula and action steps for realizing these truths."

~ Terry Tillman
http://www.227company.com

"Paul's Book, *Secrets of the Millionaire Inside,* will change the way you think about money. This book will show you how to stop wasting your time by trying to save money, and show you how to use your time to make more money."

~ Brett Goldstein, host, Your Money With Brett and Joe
www.yourmoneyshow.com

"This book shows the relationship between your thoughts and your reality and demonstrates exactly how a person must think in order to attract the life you want. But it doesn't just stop there; it provides you with 7 actionable steps you can take to make anything you want become a reality."

~ Dr. Dennis S. Reina, co-author,
award winning, business bestseller,
Trust & Betrayal in the Workplace:
Building Effective Relationships in Your Organization, 2nd ed.

SECRETS OF THE
MILLIONAIRE
INSIDE

THE 7-STEP FORMULA FOR BECOMING A MILLIONAIRE

PAUL McCORMICK

MIRACLE WRITERS LLC PUBLISHING COMPANY · SEATTLE, WA

Published by: Miracle Writers LLC Publishing Company
RCM #28550
P.O. Box 34628
Seattle, WA 98124-1628

Cover design: George Foster
Foster Covers

Editing &
Book Design: Ron Kaye & Connie L. Schmidt
Schmidt Kaye & Company Professional
Literary Services

Library of Congress Cataloging-in-Publication Data

McCormick, Paul B.
Secrets of the Millionaire Inside
ISBN-13: 978-0-9794338-4-9
LCCN: 2008905534
Category: Self-Help, Wealth

10 09 08 07 06 05 04 03 02 01
First Printing October 2008

Printed in the United States of America

Dedication

*I dedicate this book to all of you
who dare to believe
your life can become extraordinary,
and that you can become incredibly wealthy.*

*And to my wife Nicole
for being by my side for eighteen years
even during the years I thought
I had to work so hard to get rich.*

*And to my son Brandon
who changed my life
by showing me that the truth
about so many things in life
is many times hidden.*

Table of CONTENTS

*Where will you be
three years from now?
Will you still be sleepwalking
through your ordinary life,
or will you have awakened
to an extraordinary world
of infinite possibilities?*

*The world is as you dream it.
Dream small
or dream large.
It's all up to you...*

INTRODUCTION

FORMULA for an Extraordinary Life

Within the next three years, would you like to finally...

- ✦ Be financially free?
- ✦ Have all the money you want?
- ✦ Know how to make more money any time you want?
- ✦ Not have to go to work – not ever again?
- ✦ Be able to buy whatever you want, and not care what the price tag says?
- ✦ Go wherever you want, whenever you want?
- ✦ Be able to spend millions of dollars to help other people?
- ✦ Create free time for yourself by giving jobs to others?
- ✦ Get richer and richer every day?
- ✦ Get more and more free time with each new day?

Would you like to be able to buy a home in Hawaii or some other place you've fantasized about? Can you picture yourself lounging on a pristine beach, gazing out at turquoise waters, relaxing and thoroughly enjoying your life – and knowing you are making more money every hour you linger in paradise than you used to make in an entire week?

Can you imagine the luxury of being able to buy whatever you want without ever needing to look at the price tag?

"Paul, everybody has these dreams," you might be saying. "That's why there are so many late-night infomercials on TV, promising that the good life is all within reach if you only buy this or that book or program. But in reality, only a lucky few get to live this kind of life. And in the case of most of the infomercials, the only person getting rich is the person who's selling the product."

> # Ordinary people can become financially free. I did and so can you.

I don't blame you for being a little cynical, in light of all of the material that is out there telling you how to get rich overnight without lifting a finger. I certainly don't blame you for having doubts about whether *you* can be rich, given the myths and falsehoods we're all taught about money and wealth – and, for that matter, the lies we're taught about rich people. (I will discuss many of these myths and lies in this book.) Most people *don't* believe they have the ability to change their lives in the way I described. They don't think they will ever be able to have the level of wealth and freedom I'm talking about. And because they believe they have no hope of ever being wealthy, they continue to think and act in ways that will ensure their lives stay exactly the same. This only reinforces the myths and falsehoods.

Do you see what a vicious cycle it all becomes?

Cycle of the poor & middle class

1. I have no money so I have to work harder.
2. I work overtime to get more money.
3. Since I work so long I barely have time to get house hold chores done.
4. I don't have much money so I have to do all my chores myself.
5. With work and chores I have zero free time to imagine a good life.
6. Since I have zero time I can never even *think* about how to change my life
7. Since I never think about changing my life, I just keep working hard all day and doing chores when I come home.
8. I seem to get poorer and poorer as time goes on.
9. I have less and less free time as time goes on.
10. I am getting nowhere in my life.

I say it's time to break that cycle (and we'll discuss this point in more detail in Step 1). Virtually anyone can have the kind of life I'm talking about, and in this book I will show you how *you* can have it.

What you'll learn in this book

+ How to think like a millionaire
+ How to see the world as full of possibilities & opportunity
+ How to create free time
+ How to turn dreams & imagination into reality
+ How to create action plans that work
+ How to create money with only your thoughts
+ How to get richer and richer with more and more free time

It's not just about having a lot of money to buy things to satisfy all of your wants or to impress other people. That's not the way to happiness. I intend to show you how to have all the wealth you desire, but to have it in a way that makes you feel great about yourself and happy with your life – and, equally importantly, *in a way that brings value to the world around you and to the people in your life.* You will see that bringing value to the world is a very important part of this Formula. My hope is that through this book, I will inspire you to become incredibly wealthy – to gain the freedom you want in your life and create the life you've always dreamed of having.

"O.K., maybe the things you talk about are possible for really extraordinary or well-connected people," you might counter. "You know, people with lots of education or training, or people who have a wealthy benefactor. Or maybe people who are utterly ruthless, or complete workaholics, or both. But what about an ordinary achiever like me – a person who doesn't have connections, who isn't willing to cheat or step on others to get ahead, who has never had any money or any form of real success? Is it truly possible for someone like me to achieve all those things? Can I become a millionaire? Can I become financially free?"

Yes, you can, and that is what this book is all about. I will show you how to go from a place of having nothing to a place of having everything you want – not just materially, but emotionally and spiritually as well.

I will show you how to turn your ordinary life into something quite extraordinary.

Comfort and contentment are not enough

The secret to the kind of life I have, and the kind of life I want for you, is in understanding the power that you have within your mind to change two very important aspects of your life:

✦ How you view yourself

✦ How you view the world around you

As you change these aspects, the world around you begins to change in seemingly miraculous ways.

And so do you.

As the title of this book implies, the secret to becoming a millionaire, and to having the life of your dreams, lies within you. My job is to help you find and release that "millionaire inside."

> ## I don't want you to be "comfortable."
> ## I don't want you to (merely) double your income.
> ## I want much more for you than that!
> ## I'll show you how to make millions and millions of dollars, and be incredibly rich.

The important point I want you to realize is that I am not going to teach you how to have a *comfortable* life. I am not even going to teach you how to double your income. I don't want to do that – I *refuse* to do that – because I am accustomed to thinking in much bigger terms. I will teach you about how you can have an incredible life, how you can become happier than you ever imagined, and how your life can become bigger than the biggest dreams you have ever had. I'll teach you how you can have freedom that you never imagined possible. And I will teach you not how to merely double your income, but how to increase it as much as you wish. I will teach you how to become extraordinarily wealthy – how to have millions and millions of dollars, if that's what you want.

That's what this book, and all of my programs and teachings, are all about: going to the extremes with what is possible for human achievement.

Don't let that be overwhelming to you. I am an ordinary person very much like you. I didn't grow up with money. I didn't come from a place of wealth. When I was young, I was not taught any of the principles I am going to teach you. I learned them along the way, and that's how I know *they are principles – and skills – you can learn.*

The Formula I teach has seven parts – or steps, or principles, or whatever you want to call them. (When explaining about The Formula, I use "steps" and "principles" pretty much interchangeably.) You can easily learn The Formula, and if you follow it you can achieve any level of wealth you desire.

I teach The Formula in my seminars and teleseminars. I take people who are in the same place I was – ordinary people, living ordinary and often unsatisfying lives – and I teach them how to use my Formula to change their lives.

A life of comfort and contentment is fine if that's all you desire, but I have always wanted something much more for my life. My guess is that you do too, or you wouldn't have picked up this book.

What are you doing for the next three years?

I can answer that question for most people: During the next three years, most people will continue to do what they did for the last three years. They will get up in the morning. They will go through the same routine they've gone through for the last three years, a routine they could easily do in their sleep – and, in fact, it could be argued that's just what they're doing: sleep-walking through their lives. Equally as important if not more so, they will think about themselves in the same way they've been thinking about themselves for the last three years – and they will think about rich people in the same way they've always thought about rich people.

"Wait a minute, Paul!" you're saying. "What do 'most people's' opinions about rich people have to do with your point?"

Quite a lot, actually, as you'll learn a little later in this book.

During the next three years, most people will go to their jobs and spend their time all day at their normal duties, perhaps dreaming of the day when they can get a raise or a promotion, or find more fulfilling work, or retire, or simply tell their boss to take a hike. They'll go home and spend their free time the same way they always do – and for all too many people, that means whiling away hours on the sofa in front of the TV, watching sporting events or crime drama reruns or ridiculous "reality" shows or mind-numbing comedies until it's time to go to bed. Day after day, night after night, most people will continue to go through the motions, all the while trying to ignore the current of discontent that runs through their lives. They will carry on as they have for the last three years – and guess where they will be three years from now? I can almost guarantee that at the very best, they will be in the same financial situation they are today. Maybe they'll be worse off. Either way, they still won't have

the money they want, and they won't be as satisfied and happy with their lives as they wish they were.

Does this in any way describe you? Do you want to change it?

If so, how do you do it? Where do you start?

I'm glad you asked. As implied above, change is an inside job, and it starts by changing your thoughts. This is a truth that you may have heard a hundred times before, but if you are still unsatisfied with your life, I guarantee that you haven't taken this truth to heart. That millionaire inside, that happy and fulfilled person within you, can only be accessed and released if you begin by *changing your thoughts*. I intend to show you how to do just that.

When you do…

+ You will think differently about yourself.
+ You will think differently about the people around you.
+ You will think differently about your job.
+ You will think differently about rich people and how they spend their time.

"Good grief, Paul, are you still harping on what you think I think about rich people?" I can almost hear you asking. "What's your point?"

Be patient. I'll get to that later, I promise.

I am going to start with helping you change your thoughts, but that's only the beginning. I will also teach you how to begin changing how you spend your free time, so you become rich *and* happy, and, most importantly, so you develop the freedom you want in your life.

Guess where you'll be three years from now if you put my Formula into practice in your life? You will become a millionaire – at least. Three years may seem like an impossibly short period of time in which to become wealthy in the way I've described. Yet you can easily become financially independent and free in three years – if that's what you choose to do and if you're willing to do what it takes to get there.

My Formula will teach you how to focus your desires to achieve what you want, and how to use the power of your mind, your emotions and your imagination to bring almost magical opportunities into your life. So you will begin thinking like a millionaire, acting like a millionaire and them you will become a millionaire. You will then fall into the cycle that the rich are in.

FREE Report
Top 10 Money Myths
Outrageous Lies That keep Us Poor
www.FormulaForMillionaires.com

Cycle of the rich

1. Think like a millionaire.
2. Hire people to help do your chores.
3. Gain free time to imagine a better life.
4. Make an action plan.
5. Take action.
6. Manifest money from your thoughts and actions.
7. Hire more people to gain more free time.
8. Do it all again and create massive wealth.
9. Keep getting richer and richer, with more and more FREE TIME.

So if you want an answer to the question, "What are you doing for the next three years?" here it is in nutshell. You will be stuck in one of these cycles:

✦ Either the cycle of the poor and middle class – as outlined earlier – where you get poorer and poorer and have less and less free time; where you work hard and never get ahead...

✦ Or will you chose to move with me into the cycle of the rich, where you get richer and richer and have more and more free time.

It's your choice. If you want to enter cycle of the rich, it's easy: all you have to do is follow The Formula. For FREE TIPS on how to follow The Formula right now, go to my website and download "Paul's Tips on How to Become A Millionaire." (I promise it's FREE.)

Why not become rich and happy all at the same time?

In June of 2007, I had just published my first book, *Secrets Of The Miracle Inside*. To aid in promoting it, I was in New York at one of the largest publishing trade shows in the world, Book Expo America, commonly known as BEA. While there, I was privileged to meet with another bestselling author named Robert Kiyosaki, who wrote the *Rich Dad, Poor Dad* series. As you may know, this is a series of books about the philosophies and strategies of managing money. Kiyosaki deals in real estate, so many of his books are about that topic, but he also writes books for general audiences. More importantly, his work concerns not just the practical "how-to" but also the *philosophy* of developing wealth and creating money. His books are so popular that they have sold over 27 million copies.

I love Robert Kiyosaki's work, and I admire the way he has expanded the *Rich Dad, Poor Dad* brand. Most of all, I agree with his philosophies. I mention this because if you like Kiyosaki's work, you'll like the principles I teach, because even though they are not identical to his, he and I are definitely on the same page.

While I was in New York at BEA, I was invited to participate in a corporate retreat in New Orleans a few weeks later. The theme at that retreat was "The Law of Attraction." I was invited to the event because of my book, *Secrets of the Miracle Inside*. This book is about changing the way you see yourself and the world around you, and changing your life in incredible ways as a result. As such, it fit right in with the retreat's theme.

The Law Of Attraction, or LOA, is an ancient idea, newly popularized in the phenomenally successful DVD and book, *The Secret*. The idea behind LOA is that by changing how you think, and by focusing on what you want, you can attract whatever you want into your life. You can attract money, good health, good relationships – anything and everything you want in your life – by changing your thoughts.

> # There are two elements to becoming incredibly wealthy. When you mix these two elements together, the results are almost magical.

The Secret (and the Law Of Attraction) have earned nearly as much criticism as accolades. Some people think *The Secret* greatly oversimplifies or misrepresents LOA. Some say it promotes magical thinking or wishful thinking, that you can't just think good thoughts and expect life to go your way. Some criticize it for being too focused on acquiring material things.

I know from experience that having a happy life, and becoming a millionaire, *do* involve more than thinking good thoughts – but changing your thinking is an absolutely essential beginning. You also have to take action in accordance with your thoughts and desires – a point we will go into in greater detail as this book progresses – and in fact most of the teachers in *The Secret* teach this point as well, in some form. As for the focus on material gain, that was a marketing decision the producers of *The Secret* made because that's what so many people are interested in. Most people realize, and I certainly teach, that life is about so much more than the acquisition of "stuff."

The Secret does not have all of the answers, but nonetheless I found it to be a beautiful and inspiring work, and for many people it has been an excellent starting point for changing their way of looking at the world and at themselves. For many it has served as a springboard to a new life of abundance.

I was pleased to be invited to participate in that corporate retreat in New Orleans, because I knew it would be a great opportunity to share my message with a receptive audience. Also invited were two celebrity authors, speakers and entrepreneurs, John Assaraf and James Arthur Ray, who happened to be in *The Secret*. John Assaraf and James Ray are big names in the industry, even more so since the release of *The Secret*. I felt honored to participate in this event with them, and during this time I was able to gain more insight into their philosophies – insight that doesn't always come out in the media promotions about them. After this event I understood more clearly than ever that in truth, I had been successfully using the Law Of Attraction in my own life for a long time.

By meeting and working with these big names, I have also gained a greater understanding of the common thread that runs among "money people" like Robert Kiyosaki, and people who are more spirituality based, such as those who were featured in

The Secret. I find there are really more similarities than differences among these varying philosophies.

Whether you're a fan of the Law Of Attraction or Robert Kiyosaki or both, I believe that *Secrets Of The Millionaire Inside* will resonate with you, for in a sense this book combines all of these different ideas. That's because I want you to have the best of all worlds; I want you to have a balanced life where you can enjoy wealth *and* happiness. I've achieved both, and you can too.

The road to wealth as I teach it really has two components. There's the "money " component, and I will teach you step-by-step the practical principles of how to create massive amounts of money. But I also teach you about the inward journey of changing the way you think about yourself and the people around you – and about money as well.

When you mix those two elements together – the hardcore money principles and the profound change in the way you think about your life and about money – an almost magical thing happens. You will find that there are many times when money or something else you desire comes into your life, and there is a perfectly logical, explainable reason. But then there are those other times when terrific things or wonderful people appear almost as if by magic, and you honestly can't explain why it happened.

Everyday miracles

I've had it happen to me both ways. Many times when money has come pouring into my life, I can tell you exactly why and how it happened. I know full well that it happened because I made plans and I took action. Money came into my life as a result; there was no magic involved.

But I can't deny that there are other times when money has come into my life and I *can't* explain exactly why. Upon analysis, however, it always becomes clear that it happened as a result of my applying The Formula I'm going to explain in this book. On

those occasions, I didn't necessarily take any action; seemingly it "just happened." But in truth it didn't "just happen," for in all cases I did do one thing: I initiated a thought process. I *intended* for the money to come – and all of a sudden, it came.

Sheer luck? Coincidence? Or is there some scientific explanation, or perhaps some supernatural force at work in the universe? Ask ten people, and you'll probably get ten different opinions about the "why" of it. I'm not a quantum physicist or a philosopher or a theologian. I'm just a regular guy who has learned that these "everyday miracles" seem to happen more frequently when I apply The Formula to my life.

(Everyday people can make their own miracles!)

One of these "miracles" happened to me just a few months before this book went to print. I was expecting some money from a business deal, but then I began stewing over the possibility that I would get cheated out of about $50,000.00. I became quite agitated, mentally playing out a worst-case scenario over and over, formulating all possible arguments in my mind. I was thoroughly convinced that my partners in this deal were going to cheat me, and I got so absorbed in my worries that for a while, I did something I rarely do: I abandoned my own Formula.

I want to emphasize that this Formula, properly applied, does two things: it brings about peace and happiness, while at the same time bringing incredible wealth. To achieve that wealth, you don't have to argue with people, as I was imagining myself doing. You don't have to cheat, as I was imagining my partners were planning to do. You don't have to be greedy. You don't have to do or be anything that's not perfectly honest and full of integrity. When this Formula is followed properly, *all* the people involved will be happy, all will feel they've been treated fairly – and all will be wealthy.

Fortunately I stopped short before I drove myself complete-ly crazy or ended up making a big mistake. I made a conscious choice to "let go" and trust in The Formula – or the universe, if you're inclined to think that way (yes, I am). Did the story have a happy ending? It did, and a far happier one than I could have imagined during the time I was rehearsing all of those ter-rible arguments in my head. You will read more about this in-cident in Step 3. The point is that my Formula has never failed me, and it didn't fail me then, although I came close to failing *it*. In the end, I chose to let go of my worries, fears and anger – and the results, as far as I'm concerned, were nothing short of mirac-ulous. Not only was I *not* cheated out of that paltry $50,000.00; I received a jaw-dropping amount of money from the deal, much more than I had expected.

Things don't always turn out as amazingly as they did for me in this instance, but as a result of using my Formula, events have turned out extremely well for me on enough occasions that I am thoroughly convinced The Formula works. I am com-pletely certain that it's not just "luck" or coincidence.

What I will teach you throughout this book is how to cre-ate similar miracles in your own life. I'll show you how to make plans and how to take action that will directly result in bringing wealth into your life. When you learn to put this Formula into practice, don't be too surprised if you begin experiencing "bo-nus" effects as I did, where money and other good things just "show up" for unexplainable reasons.

Don't be surprised if your life becomes, like mine, an aston-ishing adventure.

Most people view their life like this:

✦ Life is hard.
✦ I must work hard.
✦ Money is not easy to make.
✦ People around me stifle my success.
✦ I never get the lucky breaks.
✦ I'll never get ahead.
✦ Getting rich is only for a few lucky snobs.

The rich view their life like this (even before they ever get rich):

✦ Life is easy.
✦ I'll find the short cuts.
✦ Money is easy to create once I know how.
✦ Nobody can stop my success, only I make it happen.
✦ I'll create the opportunities in my life.
✦ The world is full of opportunities every single day.
✦ Getting rich is a mindset – and a choice.
✦ It's easier making money than not making it.
✦ It takes less energy to become a millionaire
   than to stay poor.

A book is born

This book came into being in the fall of 2007, when I was doing a radio show in the Seattle area with Dr. Pat Baccili. She has a fabulous talk show called *The Dr. Pat Show*, on which she covers a wide range of intriguing, cutting-edge topics. On this particular show we did a two-hour segment titled, "Can you be spiritual and still love money?" You can listen to the archive of that show or listen to Dr. Pat live every weekday at www.TheDrPatShow.com.

> # For a wide range of intriguing topics, check out *The Dr. Pat Show* with Dr. Pat Baccili at www.TheDrPatShow.com.

In my work, I interact with many different types of people. Some of them are very successful and money-oriented, and some are more spiritually oriented and focused on happiness, emotional harmony, exploring the inner self, and connecting with God/Source/the spirit of the universe. I have found through my interactions with these diverse types of people that many folks seem to believe you can either be rich, or you can be happy and fulfilled – but you can't be both.

That, as I noted earlier, is far from the truth, and this is why so much of my work focuses on teaching that you can have wealth *and* happiness. I have been known to declare, "If you don't have money pouring into your life – and you want it – then *something is wrong*, and not just from a financial but from an emotional or spiritual standpoint. Something is broken that needs to be fixed, because *you should be prospering*. You *should* be happy, healthy and wealthy. *If you want more money, you should have more money!*"

Let me repeat that: If you want money and don't have it, then something is wrong, in more areas than just your finances.

> # If you want money and don't have it, then something is very wrong – not just financially – but emotionally and spiritually as well.

of the MILLIONAIRE INSIDE

If you just look at the first part of that statement, it might seem that I'm only stating the obvious. "Of *course* something is wrong, Paul, I need money and I don't have it!" If you look at the entire statement, though, it might seem pretty bold, perhaps a bit presumptuous, maybe even a little arrogant. How dare I presume to tell you that you have a cash-flow problem because something is wrong in your life emotionally and spiritually?

On the other hand, you may very well agree with me, but still feel at a loss as to what to do about it.

As you can imagine, this is a subject that strikes a chord with many people, and this was a fitting topic for Dr. Pat's show. And we *did* strike a chord that morning. We had originally intended to do a one-hour segment, but it was so popular we kept it going through the second hour. The phone lines were going wild; people continued to call long after the show, and were e-mailing both Dr. Pat and me late into the night. Several people asked me on the air if I had programs to mentor them either one-on-one or in groups, teaching them the principles of how to create wealth.

What inspired so many people to make this request were the real-life examples I shared on the air. Whenever I do a show or speaking engagement and want to illustrate a point, I talk about something that I'm going through at that time. On Dr. Pat's show I told my listeners about my plans to leave the radio station right after the show and drive over to look at a building I was planning to buy. "I'm going to go look at a piece of commercial property I'm planning to purchase," I told them. "It costs over a million dollars, but will generate income for me for the rest of my life – or as long as I own the building.

"Furthermore," I continued, "I plan to buy that building *without spending a dime of my own money*. It will provide me with enough money to buy a luxury car or anything else I want. I'll be able to buy that building, that car, whatever I want to buy… without spending any of my own money."

People were calling in and saying, "I've got to learn how to do this – you've got to do a mentoring program, a seminar, a teleseminar or something where I can learn this too!"

Six-week teleseminar
My Formula For
Becoming A Millionaire –
using real estate
as a real-life example.
www.FormulaForMillionaires.com.

Right there on the air I agreed that I would put together such a program for my listeners. It took me about a month after that show to put it together. I created a six-week teleseminar called, "Formula for Becoming A Millionaire." If you're interested, I'm still offering it. I gave the first one at the beginning of 2008, but it continues to be very popular because it teaches you step-by-step what you need to do to develop the kind of thinking necessary to become a millionaire. In that teleseminar, I use real estate as an example because that's how I'm making so much of my money these days. I teach you how you too can create wealth in real estate, even when you have no money to start with.

I knew when I launched the teleseminar in early 2008 that I was teaching more than the principles of how to create wealth in real estate. I was teaching people how to change their thinking as well. I began by exploring the way most people think about money, and how rich people think about it differently than the way poor or middle-class people do.

I was also sharing a lot of practical advice. I used the commercial property I was buying at the time as an example, explaining exactly how I did it, step by step. During this six-week teleseminar, I also found two other commercial properties that were each worth over a million dollars. I got them under contract, and my next step was to find the "free money" I would actually use to buy those properties.

During that class I was able to share real-life examples of:

✦ how to find properties

✦ how to get them under contract

✦ how to find "free money" from banks that are willing to loan you the money to buy properties that are 100% financed – so you're not spending a dime of your own money

✦ how to use those properties – to manage them and take the tax benefits the government gives you

In that teleseminar I wasn't just teaching theory; I was actively practicing what I taught. From the time the teleseminar was first conceived on the radio program until the time it ended, I acquired no less than three different commercial properties, using each one to illustrate one very feasible way you can make yourself into a millionaire.

And that teleseminar inspired this book.

In this book, I don't focus specifically on real estate, as there are a number of other ways to make money through businesses and all kinds of things you love to do. You might be a singer. You might be a musician or an artist or a writer or a person who really has a way with horses or dogs. There are all kinds of ways to take what you love to do and turn it into a multi-million dollar venture. I'll give you some great ideas as this book progresses, and I am also creating new products all the time that will help give you even more ideas, as well as show you how to implement those ideas.

If you want to know more about real estate, I urge you to take my teleseminar. If you want to learn the seven steps of The Formula to use for any area of your life, then continue reading this book, because I'm going to tell you what you need to know and do to develop mass amounts of wealth – and to do it in a way that creates enormous happiness for yourself and the people you love.

My quest for a balanced life

If you've read my previous book, *Secrets Of The Miracle Inside*, you know most of this story. I'm telling it here again for the benefit of those who don't know it, because it is pertinent to the point that I don't just talk the talk, I walk the walk.

I learned early in my life how to apply the principles that make up my Formula. They definitely contributed to my success, even when I was young. In truth, I've been using parts of The Formula since elementary school. I used it to become the first-chair trumpet player in my band class. Later in high school I used parts of this Formula to get straight A's. When I was in college I used it in competitive sports. When I was riding bicycles competitively, I used this Formula to become a winner in the races in which I participated. When I got into my career right after college, I used this Formula to become an owner of my own multi-million dollar company by the time I was 27 years old.

By the time I was 29, I was the CEO of this same company. I had everything that most people wanted. I was my own boss. I had people working for me. I had money. I had prestige. I had the position, I had power, I had what "everybody" wanted.

And yet I was miserable – emotionally and spiritually and every other way. Although I was materially wealthy, I had failed to apply those same principles to all the other areas of my life, so my physical and emotional health, and my relationships, weren't good.

I was chronically fatigued and could barely get through the day. I went from doctor to doctor, and nobody could figure out what was wrong with me. Eventually, I learned I had a bacterial infection in my blood that was incurable. I decided that the

only thing I could do was work on my own immune system and change my mental outlook.

Changing my mental outlook, however, was far easier said than done, for I was depressed, I was stressed, I was stretched to the limit. At the time I was also struggling with relationships with my business partners, and it was so bad that I hated my job – even though I was the boss! Yes, I was the CEO, but I wasn't a despot; I still had business partners, and I had "issues" with them. The whole situation was painful. I never realized that pain in my life could be so powerful.

To make things even worse, I was also struggling at home to be the parent of an autistic child. I was trying to learn how to be a good parent, to understand autism, to understand what I could do with my son to improve his condition – and things were tough.

Things were bad emotionally at work and at home, and all of this, combined with my health worries, led me to a state of despair: the proverbial dark night of the soul. I began to seriously wonder if there was a God or any kind of spiritual force anywhere in the universe. I wondered whether there was any purpose at all to my life. I reached a point when I didn't even want to live.

I still can't say exactly what kept me alive, but love played a part for sure – the love of my wife and son kept me going long enough to continue my search for answers. Eventually I was moved to look inside myself for those answers, and in time I came to realize that perhaps I needed to apply my Formula to *all* the areas of my life – not just to making money.

And that's how I was able to turn everything around.

Incredibly, when I began applying this Formula to the rest of my life, my health got better, my finances got even better than they were, and, most importantly, my relationships at work and at home began to improve.

The whole world around me began to change and get better, in ways that never failed to amaze me.

I began to see how much power I really had – maybe not the power to change the whole world, but certainly the power to turn my own world around.

By changing the thoughts I had, and putting this Formula into practice in my life, I was changing my entire life – and not just my life, but in many significant ways I was changing the people and situations around me.

What was truly incredible was that the more I put this Formula into practice, the more changes I saw. I continued to test it over and over, in an effort to determine just how much I could do to change the world around me.

I wondered how far I could go. What, I wondered, were the limits of what I could create for my life in terms of happiness, health and financial prosperity? The farther I tested the limits of this Formula, the more I realized *there are no limits to how happy you can be or how wealthy you can become.*

When you apply The Formula to your life, there truly are NO LIMITS to how happy you can be or how wealthy you can become.

This is as true for you as it is for me. When you put this Formula to work in your life, not only do you change your own life, your health and financial status, but you change the people around you and the situations around you as well.

Eventually, it became very clear to me that I wanted to bring the message of what I had learned to millions of people.

I became financially independent to the point that I no longer needed my job to be secure – and one day I simply walked away from my multi-million dollar career. This was perhaps the ultimate test to determine just how powerful my Formula was.

Did The Formula continue to work for me?

Well, during the first six months away from my job, I created more wealth in my life than I would have if I had stayed with my career. And remember, I was the CEO – the owner of a company – so I was making very good money. By leaving and relying on this Formula that you'll learn in this book, I created more wealth than I would have if I had stayed with the career.

Creating something from nothing... Shaping reality from dreams and visions...

Don't get me wrong; my career provided me with invaluable experience that I am still using. After all, I was with that company for seventeen years. During those years I was a consultant working closely with wealthy real estate investors and developers. These people were entrepreneurs, and I worked with hundreds of them and was responsible for billions of dollars worth of investments and developments. They would hire me to guide them step by step through the process of designing, obtaining permits, and constructing commercial and industrial buildings and properties. I became very well skilled in all of the practical aspects of my trade.

But there was a deeper significance to what I was doing: *I was helping people turn their dreams into reality* – taking their visions of what could be done, and bringing those visions to fruition. I helped dreams come true for hundreds of other millionaires, real estate investors and entrepreneurs.

I have, therefore, gained a massive amount of practical experience by working with all of these people and creating something from nothing, shaping reality from someone's vision. I was also doing it with over 100 of my own employees whom I helped to become successful in their own lives. And I was dong it in *my* life.

It is this foundation of experience that I bring to you in this book, *Secrets Of The Millionaire Inside*. You can believe me when I tell you that I know what it's like to start from a place of having nothing and creating wealth. I've been in the positions at the top of the ladder in the corporate world. I've also been at the bottom with the depression in my own life. I've been able to rebound from all sorts of adversity, and have come out even stronger and happier.

And so can you.

(...It all becomes effortless when you use The Formula.)

My first book, *Secrets Of The Miracle Inside*, laid the foundation for healing your life and preparing you for greatness. If you are dealing with a lot of baggage in your life –stress or anger or grief or pain – I highly recommend that you read my first book, because it will help you turn that around, preparing you for a greater and more joyful life.

This book you're reading right now is the one that takes you to the next level. It tells you step-by-step what you need to do to change your thinking, and what actions you need to take to create millions and millions of dollars in your life.

There's one point I want to make before I (finally) wrap this up and get to Step 1 in The Formula. As you read this book you will notice that I repeat some points several times. This isn't because I have a short-term memory problem or careless editors. And it's not because I think you're too dim to get it the first time. My redundancy is intentional, and it is there for two reasons: (1) to help you not only "get it," but commit it to memory; and (2) to ensure that people who habitually skip around in books and/or don't read the whole thing (and you all know who you are!) will find at least one or two of the more important points in *Secrets Of The Millionaire Inside*, no matter where they open the book.

Naturally, I'd prefer for you to read the entire book from beginning to end. I think you'll get the greatest benefit that way. But no matter where you start or finish this book, or how much or how little you read, the information is always there for you to come back to whenever you feel a need for it. And, of course, you can always visit my web site, www.FormulaForMillionaires.com.

I hope you will!

Why "the dream" eludes so many

Let's face it: most people dream of being rich and having the freedom I've been talking about. Maybe that freedom means not having to go to work every day, or maybe it simply means being able to buy a brand new car – any car you want. Maybe it simply means buying a slightly bigger house, or maybe it means being able to vacation in Hawaii, or to own your own home in Hawaii. I don't know what financial freedom means to you. I don't know what success means to you. It's different for everyone.

For most people, though, it means making more money, and for many it also means having less stress in life and having more free time. Most people want all of these things, but the sad truth is that not many people know how to create this sort of wealth and freedom in their lives.

Your parents didn't teach you how to do it. Do you know why? It's simple: if they were like most of us, *they* didn't know how.

When you go to school, your teachers don't teach you how to do it. Why? You guessed it: most of the time they don't know how either. They don't know The Formula.

And you certainly won't learn it at work from your co-workers or boss, because most people in the corporate world don't know The Formula either. (Besides, if all of the employees at your workplace knew The Formula, there might be a drastic reduction in the work force.)

The good news is that you're about to learn the secrets that can bring financial freedom as well as emotional and spiritual fulfillment. I'm going to teach you how to have it all – how to create wealth and how to be happy both in the short and long term.

> # Make more money in one night while you sleep than most people make in a week of overtime. I do... and so can you.

I've accomplished all of the things I talk about. I have wealth. I've had business success. I love Hawaii, vacationing, traveling, flying first class and buying the cars that I want. I buy commercial properties, I make money off all those properties and I love that, but I also love the fact that *I am providing value to people.* I provide places for people to live, to work and to play. I provide jobs for people, so I feel good about the things I'm doing.

And yes, when I'm sleeping at night, I am still making money. I'm making more money by the hour when I sleep than ever before when I used to have a job. When I'm vacationing in Hawaii, sitting on that gorgeous beach I described at the beginning of this chapter and enjoying the sunshine, I'm making more money every hour than I used to make when I was the CEO of a large company.

Those are the secrets I want to teach *you*: how to love your life, how to enjoy your freedom and your free time, how to provide value to the world around you so you feel good about what you're doing…and at the same time, how to make millions and millions of dollars.

The good news is that you can easily learn The Formula I use.

The even better news is that when you use it, it always works.

So what are you waiting for? Let's get started on creating your extraordinary life.

*The great paradox of wealth creation:
The more you love and chase money
the more it eludes you.*

*Learn to cherish
what is truly important
and utterly irreplaceable,
and the money will come to YOU.*

STEP 1

STOP
Loving Money

My Formula For Becoming A Millionaire includes seven steps or principles that, if you follow, will make you incredibly wealthy. Each chapter of this book focuses on one of those principles. The first of these seven principles is STOP LOVING MONEY. Among other things you will learn:

1. *Why the love of money will keep you* **poor**
2. *What truly rich people love and value* **instead** *of money*

People who are not rich have a number of incorrect beliefs about wealth and the wealthy. No doubt you share some if not all of these misconceptions. Well, I consider it my job to shake them right out of you, because you will *never* be rich unless you abandon these false beliefs – and the sooner, the better.

One of the biggest misconceptions most people have is that the rich love money. It might seem that way at times, but I'll prove to you that the rich do not love money. They value something far more important than money, and I'll tell you what it is shortly. I'll also prove to you that it is the poor and middle class who love money the most – and this, paradoxically, is precisely the reason they are poor and always will be.

Another major misconception, closely related to the one above, is that the rich are greedy, and that most of them have made their fortunes by taking from other people. My hope is that by the time you are finished with this chapter, you will clearly understand that it isn't the rich who are greedy; rather, it is the poor and middle class who are the greediest people in our society. The wealthy, by contrast, are the most generous and giving people around.

Maybe you think I'm joking. Or maybe you think I'm just another arrogant plutocrat who doesn't know what it is to struggle just to make ends meet. I assure you that neither is the case, so stay with me while I explain.

(The POOR and middle class are greediest of all!)

First of all, I am not saying that poor and middle-class people are evil. Further, I have no doubt that greedy rich people exist, and that some of them *have* made their fortunes by taking from others. And you have only to look at some of those narcissistic Hollywood "celebutantes" to see that having lots of money is no guarantee of a generous heart or a concern for the world outside oneself. However, the mere fact that a person is rich doesn't automatically mean he or she is greedy or self-centered. It certainly doesn't mean that he or she became wealthy by taking from the poor. In fact, you can become incredibly wealthy by giving – by providing value to others, instead of taking from them. I know, because I've done it. It's the only way I would ever consider being wealthy or teaching someone else to be wealthy.

Again, let me stress that poor and middle-class people are not evil, but I maintain that they *are* among the most selfish folks in our society, because for the most part they're only looking out for their own survival and that of their families. They have little left over to give to the world. Furthermore, *they* are the people who truly love and chase money.

I am very aware that this is the opposite of the way most people believe – but then again, most of the things I teach in this book and in my classes are the opposite of what most people think. Most people, however, don't understand the truth about how to become a millionaire. And that is why most people aren't rich. That's why I wrote this book.

The rich get richer...

A song called "Everybody Knows" (written by Leonard Cohen and covered some years ago by ex-Eagle Don Henley) contains lyrics that declare with a sort of cynical resignation that "the fight is fixed" because "the poor stay poor and the rich get rich."

It sure seems that way sometimes, doesn't it? Poor and middle-class people want more money, but it remains beyond their grasp. They look at the rich and think, "They have it so easy. They keep getting richer and richer, and they're hardly working at all. Most of the time, they don't even have a normal day job, and they're traveling all over the world, going to places like Hawaii and playing golf all the time."

In many cases these observations are pretty accurate. Of course, there are some incredibly wealthy entrepreneurs who always seem to be working and never take vacations. But that's their *choice*; they work because they have a real passion for what they do, not because they have to go to the office every day in order to be able to pay the bills. As for the others – the "leisure class" who continue to make money while lying on the beach or playing golf or vacationing in Italy – they are the ones who really seem to be the focus of middle-class envy.

Why does 4% of the population control 96% of all wealth?

Meanwhile the poor and middle class just keep toiling away. It does seem at times that the fight is fixed.

Just how is it that the rich survive, seemingly without putting forth much effort, and more importantly, how is it that so many of them continue to get richer and richer? Why is it that four percent of the entire population in the United States holds 96% of all the wealth in the country?

Why is it that the poor and middle class seem to perpetually struggle – working harder and harder, and barely making ends meet?

It just doesn't seem fair.

Clearly, there's something the rich know that the rest of us don't. There is something that the top four percent are wise to that the other 96% are still in the dark about.

What is it?

That's what I'm going to tell you in this book. When you follow The Formula, you too can become wealthy, and you don't have to be greedy and selfish to do it. In fact, you will be just the opposite.

Notwithstanding the fact that the rich are often generous and philanthropic, and that many rich people give far more to society than they take, many people cling to the belief that rich people got that way and stay that way by taking from the poor. In most people's minds, that's the true reason that the rich keep getting richer and richer while the poor and middle class seem to get poorer even as they continue to pursue money.

I am reminded of a cartoon…

" THE RICH ARE GETTING RICHER, THE POOR POORER.
A RAISE IN YOUR SALARY WOULD MESS THINGS UP, SIMS!"

On the surface, this is just another moderately funny little cartoon, but it has the subtle effect of reinforcing the stereotype of the "ruthless rich" and the hopeless situation of those who aren't rich but are in some way at the mercy of the rich. There are two reasons I am sharing it with you:

The first reason I present this cartoon is to remind you that *if you believe the rich get rich because they take from the poor, that belief will stop you from ever becoming wealthy.* It's not the truth, so I don't want you to believe it.

Why does it matter? If you believe the rich get rich because they take from the poor, then on a subconscious level you are programming yourself to say, "I don't want to be rich because I don't want to be greedy and selfish, or even to be perceived that way." In other words, you don't want to be the type of wealthy person you yourself may currently look upon with a mixture of loathing and (let's be honest here!) envy.

Your subconscious will take it from there, and every part of your being – body, mind, and soul – will inform you that *you don't want to be rich*. As long as you let that continue, I guarantee you *won't* become rich, for you will be sabotaging all of your efforts on a subconscious level. Very simply, you will have programmed yourself for failure.

The second reason I shared this cartoon is to drive home the point that *there is a better way to become wealthy, and it is not by taking from others*.

I'll go into more detail about this later, and will suggest ways to go about amassing wealth for yourself and at the same time creating a great amount of value for the poor and middle class – which, of course, is the complete opposite of taking from them.

The very good news here is that the "fight" is not fixed. You have the opportunity to be one of "the rich" too. You don't have to stay poor. But you *will* stay poor if you continue to believe the myths about the wealthy.

Are the rich arrogant snobs?

Consider your own stereotypes and assumptions about rich people. Perhaps the word "rich" brings to mind a person in Hollywood or in one of several affluent enclaves on the East Coast. They drive a BMW or Mercedes or Bentley and they live, of course, in a colossal mansion, nestled on a breathtaking estate with swimming pools, a private lake, and a large staff of butlers and maids and gardeners. They have private jets and they travel all around the world. Naturally, they never seem to work at a day job, except maybe to do a little wheeling and dealing over lunch. For the most part they seem to be on an endless vacation.

All too often, when you think of a person who's that rich, you automatically conclude that they became rich because they valued money above everything else, and didn't value the important things in life, such as love and friendship. To become this wealthy, you assume, these people had to have been obsessed with money – living, breathing and eating money constantly. Perhaps they own businesses where they work their employees to death, paying them a pittance while gathering massive amounts of riches for themselves.

You are convinced this is true because you've seen so many of these "types" on TV and in the movies. We all have. Never mind that yesterday's villains such as J.R. Ewing on the television series *Dallas* and Gordon Gekko in the movie *Wall Street*, not to mention the rich villains on contemporary shows, are fictional characters – caricatures, really – perhaps only loosely based on reality. They are part of our popular culture, and they all feed into what we "know" about the rich, which is that the rich became that way at the expense of others.

> # I've worked with hundreds of millionaires over the years, and contrary to the stereotype of the greedy rich, many are the most generous and giving people I've ever known.
> # They became wealthy by providing value to the world.

Want to know a secret? That simply isn't true. In my seventeen years of experience, I have had the privilege of working with hundreds of millionaires. I helped them create wealth by developing concepts to turn their dreams into realities. What I learned was that wealth came to them because *they were providing value to others first, long before they ever received a reward for themselves.*

The wealthy people I worked with were the most giving and generous people I have come across in all my work. I absolutely believe they were more the rule than the exception. On the other hand, it's the poor and middle class who are, by and large, the selfish ones. They're caught in a crazy cycle where they have no time or energy to look out for anyone except themselves. (We mentioned that "cycle" in the Introduction and will discuss it further in a little while).

If I'm stereotyping and over-generalizing, well, so be it. Consider it sort of a counter-stereotype to the "greedy rich/noble poor" concept that so many people believe, against all evidence to the contrary.

The poor love money. That's why they're POOR!

Loving money

It has been said that the love of money is the root of all evil. At best, it is an unrequited love – and to make matters worse, the more you love money and chase it, the more it seems to elude you. I guess it's human nature to want what we don't have, and the desire for money is no exception. The problem is that people who don't have money – the very people who want it the most – too often have a "poverty mentality." They love money so much they will do almost anything to get it, or to save what they have. And that is precisely the reason they will remain poor and struggling forever.

Yet most of the poor and middle class can't see this poverty mentality in themselves. They continue to believe that the rich are the greedy people in the world. They may even see themselves as somehow noble: "I might be scrambling for every penny, but hey, at least I'm not a greedy so-and-so." This mindset will stop them from ever having riches in their own lives. Riches come when you stop loving money and start placing value on the one thing that wealthy people value above all. Just what is it this thing?

That's what we'll discuss next.

The way to become rich is to spend money!

We've been taught lies

As I noted earlier, many of the things I write about in this book may be contrary to some of your most cherished beliefs. Some things I've said may seem completely counterintuitive. Well, here's another piece of wisdom that flies in the face of intuition: *The way to become rich is to spend money.*

Let me qualify that. You *don't* become rich by spending your money on just anything. You don't go out and buy a thousand bucks worth of lottery tickets, for example. More than likely that will just get you closer to the poorhouse. Instead, you spend your money in ways that *will* help make you rich. For example, *hire people to do the work you don't want to do.*

"Wait a minute," you're saying. "Hiring professionals to do something I'm not capable of doing is one thing. But if I want to have more money, why would I spend my hard-earned dollars hiring other people to do something I'm perfectly capable of doing myself? I mean, sure, I hate mowing the lawn and I don't particularly enjoy washing my car, but those are things I can handle, so why throw money down the drain?" That seems to go not only against intuition, but also against common sense.

I'll get to the answer in a little while. For now, trust me when I tell you that what you've been taught isn't always right, and common sense isn't always all that sensible. As I've said,

I'll be sharing a lot of things through this book that seem counterintuitive and that might rub you the wrong way. I sincerely hope they do, because up until now everything you've been thinking about money – and all the ways you've been acting as a result of the way you think about money – have not made you wealthy, have they? At least that's what I'm assuming; otherwise you wouldn't be reading this book.

> # Everything you've ever learned about money is exactly what's keeping you poor.

I've said it before and will say it again: *Most of the people in this world don't understand how easy it is to become a millionaire, because they believe the myths that we're all taught by society.* If you continue to believe these myths, you will never become wealthy. I consider it my duty to shake you up, ruffle your feathers, and disturb you a bit, by telling you the unvarnished truth about money.

So let's get back to that counterintuitive piece of wisdom I just shared: *Spend money to make money.* I just happen to have another cartoon that demonstrates the point I'm about to make; see the following page.

I'm not suggesting that criminal activity is okay, because it's not, of course. I'm using this cartoon only to make one point: *Wealthy people use their money to buy freedom.*

On the other hand, the vast majority of poor and middle-class people live their entire lives in a "prison" of financial worries, never realizing that they too have the power to simply walk out to freedom.

"Wouldn't you just hate not being able to afford to buy your way out of prison?"

Which leads us straight to the secret, if you will – the main point of this chapter: The rich value something far more than money. Do you know what it is?

It's their free time.

The rich value time, not money – and that, my friends, is the corollary to the first principle in The Formula, "Stop Loving Money." I don't want you to merely "stop loving money"; I want you to *start* loving something else instead: *your time.*

Why is it that the rich don't value money, but do value their time? It's because the rich know something that I hope to drive home to you during the course of this book: *They know you can create any amount of money you want for your life, and you can create it any time you want.* When you get to a point where you honestly believe this is true, you will understand that money is indeed unlimited. And you will know that you really can create any amount of money you want.

If you want to double your income, you can. If you want to triple your income, you can do that too. If you want increase your income a thousand-fold, you can do that. There's no limit to the amount of money you can create; you can have $100,000,

$1,000,000, $100,000,000, $1,000,000,000... as I said, there's no limit.

The one thing in our lives that *is* limited is our *time*. We are all running out of time. All of us have a certain amount of years that we're going to live. Maybe it's 70, 80, 100 years, maybe it's a little more or a little less – but even with the benefit of modern longevity research, there are not many things you can do to double or triple the time you have on this Earth. We all have only a certain amount of hours, days and years to live our lives.

The wealthiest people understand this principle very well, *so they don't waste any of their time.*

The RICH spend *money* to save *time*. The POOR spend *time* to save *money*.

Rich people know they can create any amount of money they want, any time they want, so they would never chose to trade their precious time just to save money, when money has no value.

You can see that this is one case where going against intuition and "common sense" is the most sensible thing you could hope to do – that is, if you want to become wealthy.

Money is unlimited and abundant

Think of money like the air you breathe. You can take a breath of air by breathing very fast or very slow; you can take however much air you want into your lungs. It doesn't matter, because it's there for the taking, and when you breathe, you don't feel like you're taking it from the person next to you, do you? Why is that? It's because there is an unlimited supply of air. If there weren't, much of the life on this planet couldn't survive.

If I want to create massive amounts of wealth, I create massive amounts of wealth!

The wealthiest people think of money like air; there's an unlimited supply. If I want to create massive amounts of wealth, then I'll create massive amounts of wealth. I know I'm not taking it away from anybody else, because – yes, you guessed it – there's an unlimited supply. I'll venture so far as to say that everybody in the world could become a billionaire if they wanted to, and the fact that they don't isn't my concern; it's *their* concern. That's the way wealthy people think about money – just like air, it's free, it's available and it's unlimited.

That's why *you must stop wasting time trying to save money.* It is freely available, so why would you spend all your time trying to get something that's always available and always free? Wealthy people value their time a lot more than money, so they concentrate on saving time.

How do they save time? They do it by spending that limitless and perennially available commodity called money. Time, on the other hand, is not limitless; time is running out.

So how might you save time? To begin with, you don't waste your time doing all the things you don't want to do. If you don't want to mow your lawn, then hire someone to mow it for you. If you don't want to wash your car, hire someone to wash your car. If you truly enjoy doing these things for the exercise or the sense of accomplishment, then they are certainly not a waste of time. But if these activities are just chores and drudgery to be gotten out of the way so you can get on with your life, then they *are* a waste of time.

So it only makes sense to pay someone else to do them.

How the wealthy spend money to save time:

+ They hire maids to take care of their homes.
+ They hire gardeners to take care of their yards.
+ They may hire butlers to answer the door.
+ They might hire people to run around doing errands for them.
+ When they fly, they might fly first class to save time waiting in line.
+ They might even have their own private jet so they don't have to go to the airport and take two hours getting "processed."
+ If they want to buy something at a store, their first concern is not how much it costs, but how close the store is. They buy from the closest store even if the price is a little higher than they would pay at a store that was further away. They would never think of driving across town just to get something for half price.

In short, wealthy people just do not spend their precious time trying to save money. They do precisely the opposite. *They spend their money every way they can in order to save time.*

Do you see the difference? It is huge. I'm really making an effort to drive this point home because most of the people in the world spend incredible amounts of time every single day doing lots of things to save just a little bit of money.

$$\left(\ \textbf{The rich spend their money every way they can in order to save time.}\ \right)$$

What class are you in – rich or poor?

In America, we pride ourselves on being a "classless" society, and to some extent we are. We don't have a caste system as in India, and (in theory, anyway) we don't put as much store on "class" as do more traditional societies such as Great Britain.

But let's not fool ourselves. There *are* different classes in this country, and in many respects they occupy completely different worlds. It is not snobbish or elitist to admit that even the most enlightened, developed society has a class system of one kind or another. We are lying to ourselves if we say there isn't one in America.

> ## There are only two "classes" of people: rich and poor

In this country we most commonly think in terms of three classes: upper class, middle class, and…well…poor (most of us don't like to use the term "lower class" because that *does* seem to have an elitist ring, and it sounds judgmental). Within these classes are various subclasses, or perhaps they are just steps on a continuum. We have people on the cusp of affluence who consider themselves to be "upper middle class." We also have the "lower middle class," or the more ambiguous "working class." Then of course there are the "working poor." (Funny how you never hear about "the lower upper class" or the "upper lower class." Maybe that's just as well!)

As you have no doubt noticed, I look at the class divisions very differently from the way most people do. I lump "poor" and "middle class" together. That's not being snobby or elitist either, just truthful. I believe that when it comes to financial well-being, there are only two classes of people in the world: rich people and poor people.

And yes, I do classify the middle class with the "poor," but not for the usual reasons that the pundits and pessimists do. It's *not* that I think the economy is going down the toilet and that the middle class is disappearing because they're all becoming "poor." I think the *existing* middle class is poor. Why are they poor? It's because *the poor and middle class have the same mentality.* They believe all of the falsehoods about money, such as:

+ Money is scarce, not abundant.
+ You must work hard to get money.
+ You have to have a job to earn money.

They believe all of this because they don't understand how wealth is created.

In these respects the poor and middle class are the same, which is why in my teachings I will continue to categorize them into one group. If you find that offensive, I don't mean it to be. I'm not making any type of moral judgment here. I'm not saying that rich people are "better" than the poor (though as a whole, the rich seem to be happier and healthier!). I am just telling you the truth about money and work, which is this: *If you have to work at your job just to earn money – and you don't get paid unless you work – then you are poor.*

Are YOU FINANCIALLY FREE?
If you have a job
and don't get paid unless you work,
then the answer is NO!
Learning The Formula can
give you financial freedom.

Before I go any further I want to briefly address this matter from a global perspective. Do not think I am implying you should not be thankful if you have a roof over your head, good food and drinkable water, clean clothes and shoes, and a relatively stable existence that isn't torn apart by famine or war. Even many of the poor in our country have a better quality of life than those in other less fortunate nations. But this really only reinforces my point: in America, we have the opportunity to have so much *more* than just a comfortable, stable life. If comfort and stability are all you want, and you don't mind being "poor" by the definition in this book, more power to you.

If you have read this far in the book, however, I suspect you want something more for your life. There's nothing wrong with that. Besides, how much comfort and stability is there in knowing that if you got laid off or "downsized," or your job got outsourced, or your company went bankrupt, you could very well be out on the streets and end up *really* poor? How much security is there in knowing that Social Security and the retirement plans you've been paying into for years probably will not come close to covering all of your living expenses in your old age?

By creating a life of wealth and freedom for yourself, you are not taking food from the tables or clothes off of the backs of anyone in this country or the poor countries of the world. To the contrary, as I've said before, the kind of wealth I teach about comes from giving – that is, *providing value* – not from taking from others. Furthermore, as I've also noted, the wealthier you get, the more you can do to make life better for the poor in this country *or* abroad, as you wish.

You sure can't do much for those less fortunate if you remain stuck in your own "prison" of financial woes.

(STOP FEELING GUILTY ABOUT YOUR DESIRE TO BE RICH.)

How much is your time worth?

Time is priceless. If you get nothing else from this chapter – or from this book – that's the one lesson I want you to take away. Unfortunately, most people treat time as if they had an infinite amount to squander. They spend their entire lives loving money and chasing money, while neglecting to love and value something far more important: their time. They will never be rich unless they *stop loving money.*

As you know, most of the people in the world are not rich. They are not rich because they *do* love money, to the point where they waste untold amounts of their precious time trying to save miniscule amounts of money. What sort of legacy will they leave for their loved ones and for the world? Probably not much of one: they will die poor and possibly in debt, having used up all of their time trying to save money in order to get ahead. They can save and save but they never *will* get ahead – because that's not how The Formula works.

That's not how the universe works.

> **Most people will never be rich unless they *stop loving money.***

There are countless ways the poor and middle class waste time trying to save money. More than likely you've never considered these activities to be a waste of time, and more than likely you've done a lot of these things yourself and see nothing wrong with them.

I'm here to shake your complacency. We are going to take a closer look at some of the ways that average, everyday people *waste time* to *save money.*

Let's consider vacations, for example. When middle-class people go on vacations, one of the things they need to figure out is how they're getting to the airport if they are flying. Or perhaps they think they can't afford to fly, so they drive – which takes even more time.

I'm not knocking the grand old American tradition of road trips. I realize that many people truly enjoy the experience of a road trip because they get to see more of our beautiful country. I'm all for that – if the trip is taken for the sheer pleasure of being on the road and seeing the sights, and is not just a miserable second choice, a massive expenditure of time to save money (although with rising gasoline prices, even a road trip isn't all that cheap these days!).

How the poor waste time to save money:

+ **clipping coupons**
+ **sending in rebates**
+ **shopping for sales**
+ **doing it yourself**
+ **walking 3 blocks to save on parking**

Even under the best of circumstances, however, road trips can be an enormous source of stress for some families. Being cooped up in a car together for days on end is not necessarily the most pleasant way for a family to spend a vacation. (I can just see some of you nodding your heads and rolling your eyes, remembering disastrous family car trips.) If you are only taking a road trip because you can't afford a means of transportation to get to your destination much faster, that makes the whole situation even worse.

So let's imagine that our family is not into road trips and they have decided to fly to their destination – say, Disneyland or Disney World. Or maybe they're just visiting relatives. One of the things they have to figure out is how they're going to get to the airport. Do they drive there and park their car in the parking garage? They could, but that costs a lot of money. Do they take the shuttle van that will pick them up at their home and take them to the airport? Granted, that's cheaper, but it takes longer – sometimes two or three hours – because usually the van has to stop and pick up several other people.

Decisions, decisions.

Many people will take the shuttle, congratulating themselves because they saved perhaps $35 compared to parking their car at the airport parking garage. They don't stop to think that they are spending two or three hours of their lives just to save $35. Without thinking twice, they've determined that their time is worth perhaps $10 or $15 per hour. Guess what? At $10 or $15 an hour, you're never going to become wealthy – not even close.

Some people take it one step further and decide they don't even want to pay for the shuttle bus, because that will cost money. Maybe they can just get a friend to take them, and they'll either pay for the friend's gas or return the favor at some time in the future. That way they still come out ahead.

> # If you don't have much money, then you may love money too much. That's exactly why you're *not rich*.

Well, that's fine, except for one thing. Now they have just cost their *friend* several hours of his or her time to come get them, drive them to the airport and drop them off. Then their friend has to drive back home. And upon their return, someone – possibly the same friend – will have to come pick them up at the airport, which will cost another several hours of that person's time. So now they're making their friend work for a pretty cheap hourly rate as well, thus helping perpetuate that poor-person mentality not only in themselves, but in their friend.

"But Paul, you can't put a price on friendship!" you might be saying, perhaps a bit indignantly. "I get the part about not wasting time to save money, but you're going a little too far here. You do things for your friends, and they do things for you. After all, isn't that what friendship is all about? It's part of the give and take of good relationships. It all works out."

First of all, I am not putting a price on friendship, which I consider to be priceless. I also recognize that sometimes there are emergency situations in which a friend needs a favor, and presumably that favor will be returned at some point. Furthermore, there are times when taking someone to the airport or running some other errand for them or with them is a way of showing love, perhaps a way to spend some quality time that you might not get to spend otherwise. Of course there's no price on that.

However, if you prevail upon someone in this way when it is not an emergency – particularly if you do it frequently – not only do you run the risk of straining the friendship, but you are demonstrating that you do not value your friend's time very highly. You are helping keep both you and your friend stuck in a poverty mentality.

Neither one of you will ever get rich unless you break out of that mentality.

Wealthy people, by contrast, would never trade their time – or their friends' time – trying to save any amount of money. Some have their own private jet close to their homes so they can just jump on and go wherever they want, whenever they want. If they're not that elaborate they'll drive their own car, park it in the parking garage for a week and pay the fee without thinking twice about it.

Once at the airport they'll zoom straight to their first-class seat, having gladly paid an extra few hundred dollars to save the time and hassle of endlessly standing in line. When they reach their destination they'll gladly pay for the fastest way – taxi, limo or rental car – to get to wherever they need to go. They will always pay for the fastest service; they will gladly spend just about any amount of money to save any amount of time.

I've given you just one example of how the vast majority of people spend their precious time trying to save small amounts of money – and, by contrast, how the wealthy minority do the reverse: they spend money to save their profoundly valuable time.

Get my FREE REPORT:
The Shocking Things We Do That Stop Us From Being Rich
www.FormulaForMillionaires.com

Why poor families stay poor

My grandmother was an inveterate coupon clipper, which nearly drove me to distraction. She died a few years ago at the age of 98, and for all practical purposes she died a poor woman. She barely achieved what I would call middle-class status; for most of her life, her financial status was closer to what most would consider lower middle class.

"Well, Paul, you just said she was practically poor," you say. "Isn't that why she clipped coupons? So what's the big deal?"

The big deal is that if you believe my grandmother clipped coupons because she didn't have money, you have it exactly backwards. I know better.

My grandmother never achieved financial strength in her life *because* she clipped coupons.

I maintain that you don't spend time trying to save money because you're poor. You're poor because you spend time trying to save money. *You're poor because of the way you think and the things you do as a result of the way you think.* Maybe you clip coupons. Maybe you mow the lawn even though you loathe that chore. Maybe you take the shuttle instead of driving your own car to the airport. All of these things add up to hours and hours of wasted time – time you will never get back. But you do all of these things because of the way you think about money.

I want you to change those thoughts now.

That will lead you to change your actions. And *that* will change your financial situation – enabling you to finally create the life you say you want.

> # People don't spend time trying to save money because they're poor. They're poor *because* they spend their time trying to save money!

I'll tell you why my grandmother's coupon clipping drove me crazy. First, she would spend a great deal of time going through the papers. That didn't affect me directly, but I did think there were better ways for her to spend her time. She would find five, six or a dozen coupons at several different stores, coupons that would save her a grand total of $3.00 to $5.00. She did this for many years. Once she got into her late 80s and 90s, she no longer drove, so on Saturdays, she would ask me to take her around to all these stores.

She always wanted to go to several different stores so she could use her coupons. I didn't want to offend her so I gamely took her, but that experience drove a lesson home to me: We were spending an extra one or two hours (at the very least) just to save a few dollars. What was that saying? As far as I'm concerned, it was teaching us that collectively, our time – maybe an hour of hers and two or more of mine – wasn't worth very much. Since she only saved $4.00 or $5.00 at the most, that meant that together we were worth about $2.00 an hour.

Two bucks an hour might well have been a living wage when my grandmother was a girl, but even then it wouldn't have made a person wealthy.

Do I begrudge the time I spent with my grandmother, taking her all around the city? Not at all. I loved her dearly and was glad to be able to help her out. However, I would have really preferred spending genuine quality time with her, doing something we both truly enjoyed, such as sitting on her porch sipping lemonade and reminiscing –rather than spending half a day going from store to store merely to save a few dollars.

My grandmother with her coupons personified the mentality of the poor and middle class. Rich people would never spend time on such things.

You have to stop doing those sorts of things if you ever want to become rich.

(If you try saving money, you'll always be poor)

My grandmother wasn't the only time-waster and money-saver in the family. When I was growing up, my father hated to pay parking meters when we went to the city. Whether it was a quarter, a dime or merely a nickel, my father loathed giving any of his money to those meters. He refused to do it. He would park three to six blocks away just to save that nickel, dime or quarter. Then we would all walk those three to six blocks to wherever we were going, and walk back when we were finished. Now, you might think that's not such a big thing; there's nothing wrong with exercise and going on a walk, provided the weather is decent and you're not trudging through a crime-ridden area in the dead of night. Many of us could probably benefit from walking more. But I say that if the only reason you're doing it is to save a quarter, then you are making a declaration that your entire family's time is worth very little.

In my family's case the walk usually took an extra fifteen minutes or so. With four people in our family, that meant my dad was declaring that our collective time was worth about a quarter an hour. It's no wonder that my father never achieved financial wealth.

If you love money so much that you're unwilling to part with a quarter to put it into the parking meter – if you think it's more important to spend your time to save ridiculously small amounts of money – you will never, ever have much money. You will always be poor, with a poor person's mentality.

Again, I'm not saying there's anything intrinsically wrong with being poor – unless you don't want to be poor.

And you don't, do you?

Thermometer for Wealth

T. Harv Eker is an entrepreneur, speaker, wealth teacher and best selling author. He says everyone has within them a financial thermostat that determines the level of wealth they will have. You set your own thermostat level based on the thoughts and beliefs you have about money:

+ how hard you believe you must work for money,
+ how to earn it
+ why the rich are rich,
+ and why you are not.

He says he can speak with anyone for five minutes and then be able to determine their financial future, simply by the way they speak and think about money.

(**For more information on T. Harv Eker, visit www.millionairemindbook.com.**)

Are the rich conceited?

Another common misconception that the poor/middle class have about the rich is that the rich are conceited, arrogant, snobbish. It's an easy assumption to make when we see the way wealthy people live – buying elaborate homes, paying for maids, servants, butlers, gardeners and pool boys, traveling in limousines and private jets – in short, the typical "lifestyle of the rich and famous." This stereotype has also been fed by fictional characters on TV; for example, who could forget Mr. and Mrs. Thurston Howell III on the 60s comedy, *Gilligan's Island*? They were complete caricatures, but not too far from what many people believe even today about the habits and attitudes of the rich.

Poor and middle class people may resent the lavish life-styles of the wealthy, in part because they're envious, but they also because they assume the rich are flaunting their wealth and wasting money. That sort of behavior seems to fly in the face of all those noble American ideals such as self-sacrifice, humility and hard work.

Naturally, many of those who are on the outside looking in, so to speak, are convinced that *they* would be the exact opposite if they had the same money. They would still clean their own floors, do all of their own shopping, mow their own lawns. More than likely, though, they'll never get to put their noble ideals to the test, because the truth is that they will never have the money. That is, they will never have the money unless they first shift their thinking, and *stop loving money*. They will never be wealthy until and unless they stop spending time to save money, and start spending money to save time.

> # The only way to make The Formula work for you is to create some free time.

Time is critically important, because you will need some time to implement the rest of the steps in The Formula. Most people don't have a lot of free time in their lives, but the only way you will make The Formula work for you is to create some free time. That's why I'm telling you right here in the first chapter – principle number one – that *you have to start spending money to save your time*.

When do you start?

How about now?

You're going to need some of that precious time to begin creating the dream you have for your life, and then to create the money and the freedom to make that dream come true. *Unfortunately, most people are so busy working their lives away that they never have to even create the dream for their lives, to say nothing of creating the life of their dreams.*

I know how easy it is to get caught up in that daily grind, that perpetual cycle that some people refer to as the rat race. Or perhaps the often-used analogy of the hamster on the wheel is even more appropriate. Some say it's just part of modern living. Call it what you will, but to me it is simply the poor/middle-class cycle. People get so caught up in this cycle that they forget they created it in the first place.

> **Most people are so busy working their lives away that they never have time to imagine how wonderful their life could be, if they only changed their thoughts and actions.**

If you're like most of the poor and middle class, you create that insane cycle without even realizing what you are doing. I gave a brief summary of this cycle in the Introduction. Let's take a closer look at how it works:

Cycles of the poor and middle class

1. You don't have any extra money – or at least not enough to cover more than the absolute necessities – so you decide you can't afford to hire people to mow your lawn, do your laundry, clean your house, wash your car, and do all of those other time-consuming chores. Therefore...

2. You have to do all of that drudge work yourself. After you get home from work at night, you have to do the chores. You have to make the food, clean the house, load up the dishwasher, wash the clothes, feed the dog, feed the cat, change the cat box, cook dinner, do the dishes, do the laundry, do the vacuuming, make the kids' school lunches, put the kids to bed, and then, finally, you go to bed. And so...

3. All you do is work, come home and work some more, go to bed, get up in the morning and go to work again. As a result...

4. You have no free time or energy to think about how to change your life. Moreover, since at a very deep level you remain unconvinced that change is even possible, you never take action to make any significant changes. So your life never changes, further reinforcing your conviction that change simply isn't possible. And before you know it...

5. Years have gone by, and you still have no money, and are still firmly convinced that the only way to get money is to go to work. Therefore...

6. You work harder and harder, hoping to get a raise, or you try to work overtime. Hence...

7. You have less and less free time, and as a consequence you have less and less time to think about how you can improve your life, and you just continue on the cycle of work and worry, work and worry...

And so on, and so on, and so on.

And there you are: caught up in the cycle. You have no time and no money, so you have to work harder and harder, doing everything yourself – and you still don't get ahead.

You're still left with no money, and no time, and very little to show for all of your hard work.

That's the cycle most people are in. They go their entire lives wondering why they work harder and harder, with longer and longer hours, getting less and less money, and still having to do everything themselves.

How do you change all that?

You use The Formula.

Fed up with the cycle of endless drudgery?
The Formula can set you free.

Cycles of the poor and middle class

Breaking free from the "poor" cycle

The rich are in a cycle of their own creation too, but it's a completely different kind of cycle. This is one that reaps benefits instead of worries and hassles. I mentioned this cycle in the Introduction as well. Let's take a closer look at it now.

Even before the rich *become* rich, they begin practicing The Formula, and they start with this very first principle: *Stop loving money*. They know their time is more valuable than money will ever be, so from the very beginning they spend money to save time. It may not be much money at first, but it's enough to save them a little time, and they use that extra time to visualize a plan for changing their lives. They know that visualization isn't enough, so they take actions to start building a better life.

$$\Big(\ \textbf{Even before the rich}\ \Big)$$

Even before the rich *become* rich, they value time more than money

As they begin to take that action they make a little money. As they begin creating a little wealth in their lives, guess what they do with that wealth? They spend it in ways to create more free time for themselves. They hire help to mow their lawn, wash their cars, do their laundry, clean their house, or whatever else they don't want to take the time to do. Guess what they do with that free time they just bought themselves? Well, they sure don't sit around watching television or clipping coupons.

They use their free time to continue to visualize an even better life for themselves and to dream even bigger dreams of what they want to do, so they can continue to put together action plans to make their visions reality. Then they take more actions and get more wealth. And what do they do with that wealth? They buy more and more free time. At some point they have so much wealth they are able to quit their jobs, and perhaps they hire more people to do all the things they don't want to do.

They hire butlers, housemaids, gardeners, pool boys, limousine drivers. They pay for first class plane tickets or they may spring for a private jet, but as they create more and more wealth for themselves, they find ways to get more and more free time. *That's* the cycle of the rich. They become richer and richer, and if they work The Formula right they have more free time… until they're incredibly rich and have an abundance of free time in their lives to do whatever they want.

I would ask you, then, to consider that all of those maids and butlers and limos and first-class tickets aren't merely ways that rich people have of flaunting wealth. Think of them instead as shrewd ways to buy more of that most precious commodity: time. Think of them as ways of ensuring that the cycle of wealth and freedom perpetuates itself.

So don't waste any more time wondering why the rich keep getting richer and the poor keep getting poorer. It is because the rich spend money to save time, and the poor do the opposite: they spend time to save money. That's why the rich get richer and the poor get poorer

If you're ever going to become rich, you must start valuing *your* time instead of money. By doing this you will soon be able to have free time *and* enormous amounts of money.

For most people this is a new concept. As we discussed in the Introduction, our parents didn't teach it to us, nor did our teachers, nor our bosses or co-workers. They didn't know The Formula.

Most of the people who raised us or taught us while we were growing up were caught in that seemingly endless cycle of work and worry and more work and more worry that the poor and middle class endure every day of their lives. That sounds pretty depressing, but it doesn't have to be, for once you know and begin practicing The Formula, it is just as easy to get caught up in the cycle of wealth and freedom and more wealth and more freedom.

Which cycle would you rather be in?

I've been in both and I *know* which one I prefer. I know which one I want to see you in too.

A free gift that will help you get wealthy

As I've said before, I have done all of the things I recommend in this book. I have developed financial freedom that allowed me to walk away from my job. I know how to create free time. I know how to create money because I've done it in my own life.

And you can be sure that I have no qualms about hiring people to make my life easier for me. I hire people to do work for me during the summer and throughout different parts of the year. I always fly first class. I spend money to save time every place I possibly can. The more I do that, the wealthier I become.

I want to teach you the same principles. Sometimes in order to change we need someone to point us in the right direction. Therefore, I'm offering a gift to you that will help you dig deeper into some of the points in this book. I have put together a free special report that includes a list of things I want you to consider, points that will help you in creating your extraordinary life. You can get this report on my website, www.FormulaForMillionaires.com.

FREE REPORT:
Lifestyles of the Affluent ~ Shocking Secrets That Make Them Rich
Go to
www.FormulaForMillionaires.com

The report goes into more detail than I've been able to go into here about the things that rich people do to spend their money to save time. All of these are things you'll want to think about doing for yourself, because the way to become rich is, simply, to begin doing these things. In the same report I have a list of the things the poor and middle class do – of how they spend their precious time trying to save money. They are the things most of us do, *but you have to learn to stop doing those things if you are ever going to become wealthy.* I urge you to go to my website and get this free report. It will help put you on the fast track to becoming wealthy.

* * * * *

There will probably always be poor people and rich people. Contrary to those song lyrics I mentioned earlier, however, the "fight" is definitely not fixed. The game of wealth building is wide open, and anyone can play to win. That includes you.

First, however, you have to *stop loving money, and start valuing time.*

Of course that is only the first part of The Formula. It's a very important principle because it starts you on the road to changing your thinking, but it's just the beginning. Step 2 will continue the process of changing your thinking about money.

So don't stop now; let's get right to it!

**The game of
wealth building
is wide open,
and anyone can
play to win.
That includes you!**

Money is not currency or coin or gold,
it's not plastic or paper
it's not stocks or bonds or certificates.
It is not a "thing"
to be relentlessly pursued
and jealously guarded once attained.

Money is a mere idea,
in a boundless world of ideas
and sometimes it only takes
one small idea
to generate boundless wealth.

STEP 2

REALIZE Money Is Just An Idea

This chapter explains the second principle in my seven-part Formula For Becoming A Millionaire: REALIZE MONEY IS JUST AN IDEA. Among other things you will learn:

> *1. That money is not an object to be pursued or a finite resource to be hoarded*
> *2. That money IS an idea that can easily be translated into reality*

Wouldn't you love to be able to create massive amounts of wealth by doing something that was actually *fun?* Wouldn't it be terrific if you didn't have to work hard to make money – if you could work at your own pace doing only the things you liked?

How would you like to work only when you wanted to work – and all the rest of the time you could relax, have fun, take vacations and simply enjoy life?

How would you like to reach the point where you had no financial stress in your life?

All of these things really are possible – and not only possible, but doable. This chapter, which discusses the second step in my seven-part Formula, will propel you further in the direction of those possibilities.

I'm not saying that you can just sit on your duff and do nothing. I am not teaching pie-in-the-sky thinking here. To the contrary, I have been and will continue to be realistic and pretty blunt with you in this book. To be anything less wouldn't be fair to you or to me. If I tell you something that's obviously not true, I lose my credibility and you won't want to buy any more of my books and other products. So I have a dog in this hunt too. The truth is that you do have to do *something* in order to reach the level of wealth and freedom I am talking about, and as this book progresses, I'll tell you what it is you have to do. What I *am* saying is that you don't have to work yourself half to death doing things you can't stand in order to make all this money.

You can actually have fun getting (and staying) rich. After all, I did (and am)!

You have to do *something* to get wealthy, but that something can be fun!

Before you *do* anything, however, you need to continue working on the way you *think*. Unless you change your thinking, you won't be able to take the kind of action you need to take in order to become incredibly wealthy. In the previous chapter, I told you to *stop loving money*. Poor and middle-class people love money, so they pursue it – and it continues to elude them. We discussed what rich people love and value far more than money: *their time*. We also discussed the mistaken ideas that most people – again, the poor and middle-class – have about money and about rich people. We talked about how having these misconceptions will keep you poor forever.

I hope I was able to convince you in that chapter that in order to get rich, you seriously need to rearrange your thinking about money. Now I'm going to continue the process I began in the last chapter by telling you some more truths about money that you need to know in order to start seeing much, much more of it in your life.

Some more myth busting

Let's look at a few more of the myths that keep so many people poor. Here are two of the biggest misconceptions that poor and middle-class people cling to regarding work and money:

1. You have to work very hard to make good money.
2. If you want more money, then you have to work smarter."

Neither of those is true.

$$\left(\begin{array}{c} \textbf{You don't have to} \\ \textbf{work harder} \\ \textbf{OR "smarter"} \\ \textbf{to be rich.} \end{array} \right)$$

The reality is that *you do not have to work hard to be wealthy or stay wealthy.* And you don't necessarily have to "work smarter" either – at least if you interpret that annoying cliché the way I do, as implying that greater intelligence is the key to success and riches.

I know many people – and you might know of a few too – who are incredibly wealthy, and they don't work nearly as hard as you do. How do they do that? They weren't all born rich; in fact, very few of them were. What do they know that we don't?

You might also know people who are incredibly rich, and yet they are, as the saying goes, not exactly the sharpest tools in the shed. You just have to assume that they were at the right place at the right time and maybe got lucky (sheer dumb luck, so to speak). Well, more than likely that's not true either.

This leads us back to the question that surely must be burning in you, as it burned in me for a long time: *Why is it that some get rich while others do not? Why is it that wealth seems to keep coming into their life no matter what they do – or don't do? Why is it that some people – and maybe not even the brightest or most talented people – seem to keep raking in the bucks without putting forth much effort at all?*

And why does everyone else – particularly you – have to work so hard day after day, year after year, for an entire lifetime, and still have nothing to show for it?

Much of the answer can be found in the principle that we're covering in this chapter, which concerns how you think about money. Chapter 1 discussed your thoughts too, but it was really more about how you *feel* about wanting money. In this chapter we're talking about where we think money comes from, what we have to do to get it, and how we create it.

Let me ask you this: Do you think about money as...

1. An object, something to be pursued, something to be held onto, or...
2. A concept, an idea?

You've probably never considered this question, but I intend to change that. There is an enormous difference between 1 and 2 above. Most people think money is an object – a physical thing to go after and to hang onto when you get it. Or it's that "thing" that burns a hole in your pocket, so you have to go out and work to get more money (and a new pocket in which to burn a hole). Either way, it all boils down to treating money as an object.

Guess what? It's not.

"Um… Paul, maybe you need to look up the word 'object,'" you're probably saying. "If this ten-dollar bill that's in my wallet isn't a physical thing, just what is it? It sure has a lot of shape and substance to be just a 'concept'."

Forget that ten-dollar bill for a moment. (Besides, if you're going to carry cash around, I'd rather your wallet be full of hundred-dollar bills!) The wealthiest people know that money is not a physical object. It's not currency or coin; it's not that piece of maxed-out plastic in your wallet; it's not even electronic funds.

At its essence, money is an idea – simply a concept. When you grasp that, you have grasped the second principal in The Formula: *Learn to think of money as an idea, not as an object.*

Why does it matter whether you think of money as an object or an idea? Simple: Your thoughts influence your actions. The way you think of money will influence how you act, and that has a direct bearing on whether you stay poor or become incredibly wealthy.

It really is your choice.

Why does it matter if you think of money as an object rather than an idea? Remember that your actions are influenced by your thoughts. Your actions are a direct result of your thoughts (or lack of thought, in some cases!). When you think of something in a certain way, or believe something to be true, then you have to act in certain ways in response to your thought or belief.

People who think money IS an object must...

✦ Find where it is and go to it

✦ Find people who have it and trade for it

✦ Work for those who have it to get some of it

✦ Sell what they have to get more of it

✦ Work harder for those who have it to get more of it

✦ Save the money they have so they don't run out of it

✦ Buy cheaper products so they don't use up all the money

✦ Withhold buying what they want, so they don't go broke

When you think of money as an object, you automatically think that if you want more money, *you have to find out where the money is.* That's what most people do when they go "get" a job. You have to find which company has a job that offers the money you want, and then you have to go to that job. In other words, you're chasing that object called money.

"Come on, Paul," you say. "I have to do something to *get* the money, don't I? It's not just going to come to me. It's an interesting notion that money is an idea, a concept – but from a practical standpoint, well... I can conceptualize in one hand and you-know-what in the other, and guess which one will fill up first?"

I'm not saying that when you merely think of money it will magically pop into your life. That's not what I mean by saying that "money is an idea." But before we talk about what I do mean, let's continue to explore the mistaken idea that money is an object, and the ways that idea prevents people from becoming rich.

As noted above, if you think money is an object, you have to go somewhere to "get" that object (legally, of course). If you're like most people, you think that a job is the only legitimate place where you can obtain that object, and if you're like many, you'll go just about anywhere to get it. You have to find the people or companies who have the money and you have to go to them. You might move across the city or across the country or maybe even across the world to get the job you want – because you think money is an object and *you* have to go to *it*.

**When you think of money as an object –
and you believe that a job
is where you go to get that object –
you'll never be wealthy!**

And once you get to the place where the money is, you have to work for it. You have to give that person or company your labor in exchange for that *thing* you want called money. Then when you get that thing called money, perhaps you want to save it, so you place it in a bank – in a savings account or certificate of deposit – or maybe you invest it in the stock market or mutual funds. But you save it and stockpile it, holding onto it and hoping it might grow, watching how you spend it so you don't run out of it – all the while thinking of it as a *thing*.

Or you spend it carelessly and then scramble for more of it, staying in that cycle of work and worry we discussed in the previous chapter – and still thinking of money as a thing. Perhaps you still entertain hopes of someday getting enough money to become reasonably wealthy – so you work harder and harder in pursuit of that thing.

But you won't become rich by doing that because that's not how money works. You don't become wealthy by treating it as an object.

Nevertheless, most people continue to think of it as an object, as a thing to be traded – and a thing that, once found, must be carefully guarded.

Does all of this sound familiar? The whole routine I've been talking about – finding a job to get money, trading your labor for money, and always, always being so careful about how you spend it, how you save, it, how you invest it? Of course these things sound familiar, because they reflect the way most of us were taught to think and behave.

What money really is

If you want to create wealth and get rich, you have to understand what money really is. Money is an idea – it's a concept – and when you finally get what that means, your life will never be the same again, because you will begin seeing opportunities to create wealth every day. The ideas will be all around you.

You might be driving on the road and see a sign about a piece of property or a job opportunity, or perhaps about something that is changing in your community – and it will spark an idea in your mind. You'll think, "Wow, I just had an idea to create value for people – and to create wealth for myself or a number of other people."

You will see opportunities every day as you're talking to people on the phone, as you're reading a book, as you're watching television, as you're at church talking to somebody.

Something will be said, and you will get an idea of how to help people, how to provide value – perhaps how to bring food, clothing or job opportunities to people. Your mind will be flooded with ideas and concepts about how to help others, and through the process, how to create wealth for yourself. But all those opportunities only come after you realize that you don't have to find who has money and trade them for it; you can simply create it through an idea and some action.

Providing value for others while creating wealth for yourself is the best of both worlds. And that's the big message I want to share with you through this book – but I'm laying the groundwork in this chapter by urging you to *begin thinking of money as an idea.*

> # Don't look for where the money is. Instead, look for clues showing you how to create money where there was none before.

Rich-minded people know money isn't an object, that it is an idea.

Let's look again at who gets rich in this society. Is it the hard-working class – the people who do grueling manual labor all of their lives? Are those the people who become rich? No, they're not.

How about the middle-class people who go to school, get a four-year degree or more advanced credentials, and then land a job in a profession such as law or engineering or medicine?

Perhaps they work hard until they retire at the age of 65 or so, and they have a comfortable life – but are these the individuals who are incredibly wealthy? No, they're not.

All of these people are like most people, in that they think of money as a thing.

If you merely want to live a comfortable life, you can do what I just described above. You can get an education. That's what I did; I got an education to become an engineer. You can get a job; that's what I did. I got out of school and started working as an engineer, and I had a comfortable job. You can easily earn $50,000 to $100,000 a year doing that sort of work – and if you have the desire to become an owner of a business that does that sort of work, you can make five times that much money – $250,000 to $500,000 a year easily.

Yes, you can live comfortably, *but that's not what I want to teach you how to do*. I don't want to live comfortably. I walked away from a career where I was living comfortably. And if you want something more, as I did, then I don't want *you* to merely live comfortably. I want to show you how to become incredibly rich, how to have unbelievable wealth – millions and millions of dollars, if you wish. I want you to get to the point where you don't need to get up and go to a job every day to get that "thing" called money.

> # I don't want you to just be "comfortable." I want you to be financially free ~ making millions & millions of dollars!

After all, there are far better ways to bring mass amounts of value to the world around you.

As I've said before, this doesn't mean you will do nothing. What it does mean is that you'll do the things you love to do, and in the process create mass amounts of wealth for yourself – while at the same time, bringing a lot of value to all the people around you.

You will do this by working from the premise that *money is an idea.*

Lessons from the farmer

How *is* wealth created? Wealth is created through the process of bringing value to others. That's it; it's as simple as that. *If you want more money, bring value to people and charge them for it; believe it or not, many people forget that last part.*

$$\left(\begin{array}{c}\textbf{To create money,}\\\textbf{create value for people --}\\\textbf{\textit{and charge them for it!}}\end{array}\right)$$

In fact, you need to put others first – and that's the key to this principle, but it's the very thing that most poor and middle-class people are simply unwilling to do. *Sometimes it requires you to provide value to others – sometimes long before getting paid yourself.*

Most people aren't willing to do that. They would rather retain the poor/middle-class mentality that dictates "a good day's work for a good day's wage."

I thought that way for much of my life, so I'm not condemning it. But the wealthy know that real wealth doesn't operate that way. The wealthy know that real wealth comes when you remember the analogy of the farmer.

The farmer plants seeds, knowing that he's not going to get a crop the same day he plants it. He's not going to get a crop the next day, the next week or the next month – but in the right season of time, he will be rewarded for the work he puts in.

That's the same attitude that the truly rich have about wealth building.

> # The wealthy bring value to others long before they need to be paid themselves.

You go about providing value to the world by selling products or services or both – but the point is that you will reward those people first by providing them with the services or products they want. It may be days, weeks or months – and sometimes even years – before you will be rewarded for your efforts.

The wealthiest people are willing to do that, whereas the poor and middle class are not. That is one of the big differences between what the wealthy do and what everybody else does. *The wealthy bring value to others long before they need to be paid themselves.*

I can hear you now. "Wait just a moment, Paul. Obviously a person has to have SOME money coming in to survive while building up for that big reward. Not everyone can afford to wait months or years before getting paid. For some people it's really kind of a Catch-22 situation: if you don't have any money at all, how can you *get* the money? Can you really start from nothing and build incredible wealth? Even providing a product or service takes some money to get started – setting up an office, setting up facilities to create the product…and so on. Maybe 'the wealthy' can afford not to be paid for a while because they already have money to live on. What about the rest of us?"

These are all excellent points, and I'm going to address them later in this chapter and in subsequent chapters as well. Of course I'm not saying you can live on air and promises while you're waiting for your big payoff.

And believe me, I do understand the plight of the person who has nothing or nearly nothing to start with. We all want security, and most of us have some level of fear about having enough money to live. The difference between the rich and everyone else is how we respond to that fear. The rich run away from jobs, and run toward creating massive amounts of wealth by using the Formula I'm sharing with you. The poor and middle class, when they want to be secure and fear not having money, run to a job. But ironically, the job cannot provide the true financial security most people want. So we all want security and at first fear not having it. The difference in how we respond to that fear is what separates the wealthy from everyone else. The point I want to make here and now is that no matter who you are, no matter how much or how little you start out with, *the way to get incredibly wealthy is by bringing value to others.*

> # When you fear not having money, do you run to a job, as the poor do? Or run AWAY from jobs, as the rich do?

So what do I mean by "bringing value to others?" There are countless ways to bring value through products or services. Let's look at products first. Everything you own in your house – computers, fax machines, phones, printers, televisions, dishwashers, your washer and dryer, clothes, toys, groceries – all of these are all products you buy. Somebody is providing those products. There are farmers who grow the food, truck drivers who deliver it to the stores, and stores who work to sell it to you.

People are providing products to you, and through that process, *some* people along the way are getting wealthy – but not all of them, of course. However, if you follow my Formula when you provide products and services, you can create wealth for yourself along the way.

Let's look at some examples of services. When someone cuts your hair, they're providing a service for you. When you go to the dentist, people clean and examine your teeth; that's a service. If you get your clothes hemmed or altered and you hire someone to do that, they're providing a service to you. Your phone provider is providing a phone service for you, as is your Internet provider if you pay to be online. If you take your car to get the oil changed, somebody changes the oil for you. You're not buying a product; you're buying a service. I think you get the idea; you purchase many services on a daily basis.

> **There are countless ways to provide value – through products, services, or some combination. And there is enormous potential to become incredibly wealthy.**

The reason I seem to be stating the obvious is that I want you to think – really think – about the many different products and services you purchase to make your life easier and more comfortable.

And then I want you to think about this: Through the process of providing a product or service for people – providing something of value – there is enormous potential to become incredibly wealthy.

If you don't believe me, think about a person such as Bill Gates, who, as it happens, is providing both services and products to people. If you think about it, software is a service as much as a product – and it is one that provides value for the world, and is creating seemingly limitless wealth for Bill Gates and a number of other people.

Television shows and movies are another source of products and services provided to a number of people for entertainment. And a large number of people who are involved with the production of movies and television – not to mention the actors in the programs and films – create wealth for themselves.

> # NEED SOME BRIGHT IDEAS?
> ## Visit my web site,
> ## Download my FREE Report
> ### *Top 10 Ways*
> ### *To Create Wealth*
> ## www.FormulaForMillionaires.com,
> ## for updates.

"All right, Paul, stop teasing me," you're saying. "Bill Gates is a pretty extreme example – a fluke, maybe – and not everybody can be Bill Gates. Nor can everyone be a Steven Spielberg or a bigwig TV producer or a George Clooney or Julia Roberts."

No, not everyone can be Bill Gates, but he's far from a fluke. Not everyone can or even wants to be an entertainment media mogul or an actor. But there are countless other ways to get rich providing products and services – providing value – to a large number of people. I am constantly creating new reports, e-books and other products to teach you about *specific* ways you can provide value for others and create incredible wealth for yourself along the way. Visit my web site, www.FormulaFor-Millionaires.com, for updates.

Whatever you decide to do, however you decide to provide value to the world, think of yourself as a farmer, planting seeds for an abundant harvest in the future.

The big "yeah-but..."

I've breezed through a list of many of the products and services we all use on a day-to-day basis, and I've told you that you can become wealthy by providing a product or service. Maybe you think I'm glossing over the very obvious fact that *not everybody who provides a service or a product is becoming wealthy from doing that*. In fact, the vast majority of producers and providers are still stuck in that poor/middle-class rut.

We have doctors, lawyers, engineers and schoolteachers – all of these people are providing services, and yet few of them are wealthy beyond belief. Many are not even particularly affluent. We also have people selling products of all kinds. Most of us have friends who have small businesses – a clothing store, bookstore or some other business. Maybe you're a small business owner yourself. The point is that we all know many people who sell products and/or offer services, but are emphatically not wealthy. (And speaking of farmers, many if not most farmers are struggling too, unless they're involved in some huge agribusiness concern.)

All of these folks may be barely making a living or they might be making a pretty comfortable living, but they're not incredibly wealthy. Why is it, then, that some people provide services and products and become incredibly wealthy – and then we know a number of other people who provide services and products who are not?

You might think that the wealth-producing potential of a product or service is dependent largely upon market conditions. If there's a large demand for a product or service, it will do very well and can make its producer or provider extremely wealthy. If the market is glutted, or if the product or service falls out of favor for some reason, it won't do well. Good marketing and advertising can *create* a demand, and excellent marketing and advertising can create a huge demand – but in the end, whether or not someone becomes wealthy by providing a particular product or service is dependent upon market conditions and other factors that may be quite beyond an individual's control.

> # Anyone thinking money is an object to be found or traded *WILL NEVER GET RICH.* Realizing money is created out of nothing but ideas *WILL MAKE YOU RICH.*

That's what a lot of folks would tell you, anyway. Granted, in order to provide value on a scale that will get you wealthy, you have to pay attention to the market. You have to be aware of what people are needing or wanting at any given time, and be ready to jump on an opportunity to fill that need.

However, all of this talk about market conditions doesn't really explain why some service or product providers become very wealthy, while others who are producing the same type of product or service remain stuck in that poor/middle-class cycle of work and worry. It doesn't address the root cause. There is something more profound at work here, and I bet you've already guessed what it is.

The real difference between the not-so-wealthy and the truly rich lies in how they think about money: is it an object or is it an idea?

Those people who think about money as an object – and that's most people – will never become wealthy. It doesn't matter if you're a lawyer, engineer, schoolteacher or a dentist – if you're providing a service to people and you think money is an object, then your standard operating procedure is this: "I trade my time for your money. I work on you or for you and I charge you $30, $50 or $100 an hour – maybe $200 or $300 per hour."

Either way you'll never become wealthy when you have to trade your time in exchange for this object, this thing called money.

In Step 1 we discussed how valuable time is. You only have so much time – and I don't care if you make $200 an hour every hour you work, you'll live comfortably, but you'll never become incredibly rich.

When you sell products and you think money is an object, you run your business the same way. You make products and then you try to figure out, "How much money do I need to trade in exchange for this object to cover my time and my costs?"

If you continue to think that way, you will never become incredibly rich. Money and wealth are created in your mind by the ideas you have. In a very real sense, then, *money is an idea.*

If you give me any business, I can run it one way and not become rich – or I can run it another way and become incredibly wealthy. The difference lies in how I think about the business – which comes back to how I think about money.

Virtually everybody in our culture is exposed to more or less the same opportunities and experiences. You and I go to the same stores. We watch the same television shows and many of the same movies. We interact with many people in our social functions, whether through our rotary or church groups or business associations. We meet other parents at the soccer field or at school. We drive on the same roads. We see the same signs and billboards, so we're exposed to more or less the same world and roughly the same number of opportunities.

But 96% of the people in our world think about money as an object – and because of that, they will not think about all of the available opportunities in the same way that the wealthy person will.

The wealthiest – and I dare say the happiest – individuals in the world realize that money is an idea, shaped by all the other ideas in your mind. And ideas are everywhere! Here's a scenario that may sound idealistic, but it is reality for many people, and it can be for you too.

When you see a billboard or television show, when you read something in the newspaper or in a book, you think of a potential business opportunity, and you create an idea in your mind about what to do with that particular opportunity.

> # Why do people work a job they hate to stay poor when they could do what they love and get rich?

You think of many ways you can create wealth, and then you pick those you want to follow up on. You get in the habit of concentrating only on the things that truly interest you, and you go about creating wealth in your life doing only those things you absolutely love to do. As you get richer and richer, you find that you have more and more free time. You're not spending all of your time working unless you want to – and since you're getting wealthy doing what you love doing, even when you're working, it doesn't really seem like work.

Sounds like a great way to live, doesn't it? I can tell you from experience that it is. And sometimes it can be astoundingly easy, for in truth, a very small idea can be worth millions of dollars. The best part is that you don't have to go to a job and work every day to create those millions.

On the other hand, people who think about money as an object will continually be slaves to the idea that you have to go to work every day, providing a product or a service to people in exchange for the money you want.

Clearly, when you believe money is an object, you will never have freedom in your life, because you will be bound by the mistaken belief that you must work every day you want to be paid, and that the day you stop working is the day you will stop being paid.

Rich people know it doesn't need to be that way. You don't need to work to become rich; all you need to do is use your mind and create ideas.

Again – and I can't emphasize this enough – I'm not saying you don't have to take action. You do, and I'll tell you in later chapters exactly how you go about doing that. Suffice to say now that you do need to take action if you're going to create wealth, because you need to follow through with the ideas that you have – but *you don't have to work hard.*

Truly, the hardest work I know is having to get up every day and go to a job working for someone else. *That's* hard work, and I think you'd agree with me.

"But I don't need to be rich!"

I know a lot of people who say, "I don't need to be rich. I have enough money now and I like my life just the way it is. I'm comfortable. I'm happy with my lifestyle. In fact, I don't think anyone needs to be rich."

Do you know what I say to that? I say, "Give me a break – I don't believe it." I certainly won't believe *you* if you've come this far in the book and are still telling me you don't really want to be rich. I told you in the Introduction that there's nothing *wrong* with merely being comfortable or contented. I repeated that in Chapter 1. And I think I've said it a time or two in this chapter too.

So why are you still with me? Yep, I thought so.

You want to be rich.

I believe nearly everybody wants or needs more money. Why do I say that? Well, for starters, the people who protest most vehemently that they don't need to be rich are the same people who complain about the price of gasoline. They are the same people who complain about how much tax the government is taking from them every year. They moan about how much the cost of utilities is going up and how terrible it is that the small cost-of-living increase in their salary isn't keeping up with rising insurance, food and housing costs. The same people who say "I don't need more money" are usually the loudest complainers about how much everything costs.

> # When people say, "I don't need more money," my response is, "I don't believe you!"

I *know* they want more money, because they are scarcely able to pay taxes, utilities, gasoline cost increases and everything else that is going up and up and up. So when people say, "I don't need more money; I'm comfortable," I say, "I don't believe you."

There's something else about the people who need and want more money, even though they may not always be completely honest with themselves or others about that need. I mentioned this point in Chapter 1 but I think it bears repeating here: *The poor and middle class are the truly selfish people in our society, because they're only helping themselves.* They have no financial resources to help others. In fact, most people barely scrape by with enough money to feed, clothe and provide housing for themselves and their families. If I ask you, "When was the last time you provided housing for somebody else for an entire year?" what would you say? Most people have never done that. When is the last time you provided food for somebody outside your family for an entire year? Most people have not done that either. When have you provided clothing, entertainment or healthcare needs for someone else outside your family for an entire year? Most people, if truthful, would say, "Never."

I have an interesting surprise for you. Most of the wealthiest people provide many of those things to many people all the time. I'm not talking about sponsoring a single needy child in a poor country. I'm talking about providing these goods or services for many people, right here in our country.

The wealthiest people provide value to a large number of people.

The wealthiest individuals do this in a number of ways. One way might be through businesses that wealthy people own. They own retail stores, manufacturing companies or transportation companies. Or perhaps they own the buildings that house these companies. Every store you go in, such as a grocery store or clothing store, is in a building that is owned by somebody who is providing a place for that store to lease. Some of these facilities are owned by public companies and some by private firms. I'm not necessarily making a distinction between those, but the point is that there are wealthy people somewhere in the mix! The wealthiest people provide places for others to work, live and play. They provide apartment buildings for people to live in. They provide condos for people to buy. The wealthiest people provide entertainment centers like movie theaters for you to go to, places for you to enjoy yourself in your free time. In other words, the wealthiest people are providing a number of services to all of us on all levels. They're *providing value* to a large number of people all the time – hundreds and thousands of people – every day and all year long.

> # If you're not RICH, something is wrong. You should WANT it!

This doesn't mean they're all altruistic souls providing these things out of the goodness of their hearts. I am not trying to make the wealthy out to be saints, any more than I am trying to paint the poor and middle class as evil. We all know better, on both counts. However, altruism isn't the issue here. What's important is that regardless of how noble or selfish their motives may be, *the very wealthy are providing value for large numbers of people.*

I happen to love working in real estate, and I own numerous properties. I own commercial office buildings and I own apartment buildings. When I buy multi-million dollar apartment buildings, I buy them from developers, or from contractors, or from previous owners. Every time I buy a building, I am encouraging a developer and contractor to go build another one, because, of course, that is what they do – contractors and developers build properties for other people to buy.

So when they build an apartment building and I buy that apartment building from them for millions of dollars, I'm giving them the money to go build again – and by doing so, they employ hundreds of contractors and laborers. Therefore, I'm providing jobs for all of those people.

Then there are warehouse companies who have to store the lumber and steel that will be used in the construction of that next building. So I'm providing jobs for truck drivers, warehouse workers, construction workers and laborers every time I buy millions of dollars of real estate. In other words, I am encouraging the creation of many jobs for many people. And once I own that building, I'm providing living spaces or work spaces for a large number of people as well.

Of course, they pay me rent, but in return they get something of immense value to them. These are people who perhaps are not able to afford to buy a house at this point in their lives, or maybe they've just chosen a low-maintenance lifestyle where they can live downtown in an urban environment, and they have chosen to live in an apartment building. They'll gladly compensate me for the cost of owning that building; they pay me through rent. In essence, I'm providing a place for these people, fulfilling a need they will have for years and years to come.

Typically, therefore, the wealthiest people create jobs and living spaces for hundreds of people on a yearly basis – either directly, through owning a business and employing individuals, or indirectly, as I just described. It might be that you're providing clothing or food for people if you're in the retail or food industry business. But are you doing it on a large enough scale to make you wealthy?

> # The poor and middle class are selfish and greedy, because they are not creating the abundance they *could* be creating to help lots of people.

The wealthiest people *are* providing value on a large scale, selling services and products to a very large group of people on a continual basis – and that is the bottom line. If you want to create wealth, that's what it comes down to: you have to decide what sort of value you're going to bring the world. Are you going to bring a service to them or are you going to bring a product to them – or both? If you want to get wealthy from that, you cannot do it by giving it to one person, or to five or ten people. You have to give it to hundreds, thousands or even millions of people if you want to create wealth for yourself. (We'll go into more detail about this in Step 6.)

To me, the most enjoyable thing about having mass amounts of money is that I get to create jobs for other people. I bring value to other people. I create places for people to work, live and play. And I hire all kinds of people on a regular basis through all the work I do.

When I fly, I'm providing jobs for people who work in the airlines. When I go into hotels, I pay them exorbitant fees to stay in these luxury accommodations, and they make good money off of me. I'm glad to pay enormous amounts of money, because I know I'm helping people have wonderful jobs and make a good living at it.

So when people say, "I don't need to be rich; I can get by with the money I have," I say, "That's selfish; you should want money. You should want money so you can help other people. That's why *I* want money. I don't want money for selfish reasons. Sure, I'll buy a nice car or an expensive toy on occasion. I'll buy my wife and kid nice things. I enjoy staying at a fine hotel or eating at a five-star restaurant. But I've said it before and I'll say it again: the wealthiest people in the world are generally not the greedy ones; they are the most giving, generous people there are."

They've learned the secret – that in order to acquire wealth you first have to learn to give enormous value to a large number of people, and not have to get paid right away in order for you to offer that value. By doing this – and by using the rest of The Formula that we will be talking about throughout this book – you can guarantee yourself financial freedom and incredible amounts of wealth.

> # Don't tell me you don't want to be rich. I'm not buying it!

Rich Dude versus Average Joe

Okay, so we've established that you want to be rich after all. Don't worry; I'm not going to leave you hanging. I'm going to tell you all of the things you need to do to acquire wealth – I promise! – but first, to close out this chapter, I want to tell you a story. This is a fable illustrating how money is an idea, and how treating it that way, rather than as an object, will make the difference between moderate success and wealth beyond belief. It will also point to answers to the questions asked earlier in this chapter, regarding whether or not it really is possible to "start from nothing."

There was once a very poor village in a remote part of the world. The water source in the village became contaminated, and the nearest drinkable water was a couple of miles away. The tribal council got together and decided to offer a financial incentive for the person who could figure out how to get the water to their village.

Two of the tribal members came forward and said they were interested in taking on the challenge, so the city hired them. They worked under a contract stipulating that they would be paid so much money for every bucket of water they could transport into the city.

We'll call the first gentleman Average Joe. I think you can guess why: he thought like the average person who considers money to be an object, a thing to be pursued or traded.

We'll call the second man Rich Dude, for the obvious reason that he understood the difference. He was one of the two to four percent of people who understood that money isn't an object, but an idea.

The first thing that Average Joe did was run out, borrow a couple of buckets from a neighbor, and set to work. He walked two miles, filled up his buckets, came back and got paid immediately. Since money was an object to him, he had to trade for it. "In fact," he said, "I'm only willing to work if you pay me right away."

"Fair enough," said the village council. So Average Joe emptied his buckets, got paid, walked the two miles back to the water source, filled the buckets, came back, emptied his buckets and got paid again.

And so it went; he walked back and forth, back and forth, back and forth – two miles per trip, all day long. It was tiring work but the pay was steady. As promised, he had begun making money right off the bat, and he kept on making money.

The second guy, Rich Dude, was taking his time getting started. First he went into his hut, sat on his thinking mat, and began...well...thinking. He sat there thinking and thinking, and meanwhile there was Average Joe going by nearly every hour during the day and into the evening, toting his couple bucket loads of water.

He had to pass Rich Dude's house, and every time he looked in he would see Rich Dude sitting there in the chair doing nothing – or at least it looked like nothing to Average Joe.

Average Joe was actually getting a little smug about all of this, because Rich Dude obviously wasn't earning any money just sitting there, whereas Joe continued to rake it in steadily.

By the end of the first day, Average Joe had a pile of money in his hand, and Rich Dude had none.

On the second day it was the same thing. Average Joe got up and started working – going back and forth, back and forth, back and forth. It was on this day that Rich Dude finally came out of his house and left to go on a trip. He didn't tell anyone where he was going, and he was gone for several days.

In the meantime, Average Joe was still working steadily. With some of his money he bought a couple of extra buckets, just in case his first buckets got damaged.

By the end of the fifth day, Average Joe was racking up the dollars, making a better living than he'd ever made. But where was Rich Dude?

A couple of weeks passed and finally Rich Dude came home, and, of course, he still hadn't made any money delivering water to his village. Contrary to appearances, however, he hadn't been sitting around doing nothing. Rich Dude had been thinking, because he knew money is a concept, an idea. He knew he could have done the same thing as Average Joe, but he also knew that this was thinking about money the wrong way.

He knew he could work and get paid, but what happened if he got hurt or became ill? That would mean he couldn't earn any more money. He also knew he was only going to get paid as long as he worked, and when he quit working he was not going to get paid any more. He thought, "I don't want to do that. First of all, hauling buckets of water is hard and tedious work, and there are lots of ways I'd rather be spending my time. Second, I don't want to be compelled to work to earn my money.

That's why he spent the first day not toting buckets of water for pay, but thinking about what he could do with this opportunity.

He came up with an idea. "If I could build myself a piping system that would convey the water from two miles away into the *city, then it would operate on its own without my having to go back and forth with buckets."*

He also knew there might have to be pumps that would pump the water through the pipes, and that creating this system would entail a rather large expense.

So off he went on his business trip. He traveled into the nearest big city and visited banks and investors, proposing his idea to them. He showed them that he was under contract with his village to be paid a certain amount of money for every gallon he brought into that village. He demonstrated how, if he could create a pipeline and a system of pumps, this would generate a large amount of revenue for his investors and he would be able to pay back the bank.

He gained the support of the investors, he got the bank loan, and then he went out into the city. For the next several days he talked to contractors who might be willing to build this pipeline and pump system. He showed them that he had the financial backing of investors and the banks, so he secured an agreement with a contractor who was willing to do the work.

This entire trip took a few weeks. Meanwhile, Average Joe continued going back and forth to earn money every day, making a good wage for a good day's work. Here was Rich Dude; an entire month had gone by and he hadn't earned a dime. In the eyes of Average Joe, Rich Dude was still sitting around doing nothing, but Rich Dude knew better.

> # The poor stay poor by working hard to bring value to themselves. The rich get rich by imagining how to bring value to others.

Instead of chasing money like it was a thing to be pursued and captured, he was generating ideas to create millions and millions of dollars for the rest of his life without having to work. Sure, he had to have a worthy idea in the first place – an idea of how to meet the needs of the people in his village. And he certainly had to take action. He had to go to the bank, get investors to support him, line up contractors. Contrary to appearances, he had been taking action the entire time, but it was a different kind of action than the slow and steady work of Average Joe.

Rich Dude got the money from the bank, and the contractor he had hired began to build. It took months to build the pipeline, install the pumps and get the whole thing up and working, but after several months the system was completed. Then it was tested and approved by the health authorities to ensure the cleanliness of the water. It took a couple more months before the system was completely operational.

After six months, Average Joe had earned a half year's wage for the physical labor he had done – and Rich Dude had absolutely nothing to show for his own efforts. All he had was a mortgage he owed to the bank and a debt to investors – and he hadn't earned a single dollar yet. Average Joe was getting more than a little smug now.

> # The rich and the poor look at the same opportunities, but they see those opportunities differently, and take different actions.

Finally, though, the pumps were turned on and the water began to flow through the pipeline to the village into the reservoir that was built in the city. A meter on the reservoir calculated the gallons of water going into it. On the first day the reservoir was filled up, and at that point the village had to pay Rich Dude a lot of money. But they were happy to pay the money, because Rich Dude had figured out how to provide incredible value to the village.

What Rich Dude did next was think of another idea, for once he truly understood how ideas generate wealth, he just couldn't stop thinking of new opportunities. The ideas flowed like the gallons of glorious fresh water provided by his ingenious pipeline. Thinking up new ideas was easy. It was exciting. It was addicting.

Rich Dude went to the village leaders and said, "I understand I have this contract with you, but I'm willing to drop my rate-per-gallon by half if you'll give me a ten-year contract. The tribal elders met and they agreed. In fact they were more than happy to pay the current rate. If they could lock in ten years of reliable service with quality water provided to the city at half the rate, you bet they were willing to do it. And they were working with a known quantity. They knew from this man's ingenuity and ability to obtain financing and construction that they were in good hands.

So they gave Rich Dude a contract to provide water to the city for the next ten years – and even at the rate of half price, Rich Dude would make more money every day than Average Joe had made in his six months of providing manual labor. In fact, Average Joe eventually lost his job, because his contract was not renewed. He was too expensive and not nearly as efficient.

Average Joe was now physically, mentally and emotionally worn out, and jobless to boot. And what was Rich Dude doing? He was traveling around enjoying himself, because he had incredible amounts of money coming in. Every day he was making money.

While he was sleeping, water was flowing through the pipes, the meter was calculating the amount of gallons coming into the city, and Rich Dude was becoming Richer Dude by the hour. He was being paid 24 hours a day, seven days a week, while he wasn't even there working. While he was vacationing wherever he wished, he was being paid – making incredible amounts of money.

He was also still thinking of new things. He was thinking, "If this worked in one village, how many other villages are there in this country that need water in the same way?" So he began creating a plan to figure out where those villages were, and he began taking action to go to those villages – talking to council members in each one to find out if they needed water to be brought to their village.

He found many of them to have the same need, so he showed them what he had done in his own village, how he had created a pipeline, obtained financing and taken care of the construction – providing the quality water to all the people. He convinced most of these villages to give him a ten-year contract to do the same thing.

Rich Dude, you see, provided value to people in a large way – and he became incredibly wealthy from it.

The moral of the story, of course, is this: When you think about money as an object the way Average Joe did – and the way most people do – you believe you have to work hard for it. In the end, you are mentally stressed and physically exhausted and you will never become wealthy. It's like the lyrics to that old Hoyt Axton song: "Work your fingers to the bone and what do you get? Bony fingers!"

There are other lessons to be learned in this little fable as well. Despite the name we gave him in the story, Rich Dude didn't start out rich. He was as poor as any of the other residents in that humble little village. With his own resources he could barely have afforded a couple of buckets, to say nothing of the materials, labor and other costs to build a pump system and a two-mile-long pipeline.

But Rich Dude had something far more valuable than a couple of buckets or the money to buy those buckets. He had a brilliant idea for bringing value to his fellow villagers, and he had the unwavering conviction that he could turn his idea into more money than Average Joe could ever even imagine. Did Rich Dude just sit on his behind doing nothing, congratulating himself on his bright idea and dreaming about the money it would bring in? It sure *looked* as if he was doing nothing whenever Average Joe passed his hut that first day. And it's true that Rich Dude did do some sitting and dreaming at first.

Then he took action. He didn't have any money of his own, but he went into town and found people who *did* have money – and he sold them on his idea. After building both wealth and credibility, he was subsequently able to sell the tribe on the idea of giving him a ten-year contract. A little more wealth, a little more credibility (not to mention a lot more free time!)…and he was able to take his idea to other villages and sell them on it too.

Rich Dude knew a secret: if money is an idea, then the reverse is also true – *ideas are money.*

$$\left(\begin{array}{c} \textbf{Ideas create money,} \\ \textbf{and} \\ \textbf{IDEAS ARE FREE.} \end{array} \right)$$

Some of you are probably going to want to remind me that this is a fable – inspiring, perhaps, but how practical is it in everyday life? "In the real world – the modern world, not some remote fictional village – I'm not going to be hit with such a simple and straightforward opportunity to bring value to others as Rich Dude was." Well, don't be so certain about that. Our modern world is indeed complex, but its very complexity causes us

to sometimes overlook the simplest and most obvious ideas to provide value and build wealth. Really, all it takes is a little creativity. However, in order to unleash that creativity, you have to – you guessed it! – change the way you think about money.

When you change the way you think about money – when you begin thinking about money as an idea – you can become incredibly wealthy without needing to work hard.

Once you accept the fact that money is not an object, you are well on your way to reaching the point in your life where you can truthfully say, "Money is no object" – and *that* has an entirely different meaning!

* * * * *

Now that we've laid the foundation for changing the way you feel and think about money and wealth, and about rich people and those who are not so rich, things are going to start getting more fun. So far we've only discussed two steps in The Formula. The third step – the one we're going to cover next – will help you focus your desires and your energy, thus taking you further on the road to creating your extraordinary life.

When you change the way you think about money, you can become incredibly wealthy without working hard. Money will truly be "no object!"

*Desire alone is not enough
to bring dreams to fruition.
You have to focus your desires.*

*There is a vast and profound power ~
call it God, or Source,
or universal consciousness ~*

*Call it what you will,
but THIS is the power that gives you
the strength & focus you need
to create your extraordinary life.*

STEP 3

FOCUS
Your Desire

This chapter explains the third step in my seven-part Formula For Becoming A Millionaire: FOCUS YOUR DESIRE. Among other things you will learn:

1. *How to put your energy and attention into what you want*
2. *The power of emotion mixed with desire*

You've probably heard some variation of the story about the mother whose baby became trapped under a car when the car was jacked up for a tire change. The story goes that the jack tipped over, trapping the baby. In that moment of sheer terror, the mother, without thinking, grabbed onto the bumper of the car and lifted with all her strength, hoisting the vehicle off of the baby and saving its life.

I did some research on this, and it turns out that nobody has ever been able to substantiate that particular incident. In fact, there's not even a consensus on the details; there are a number of variations on the make of the car, the weight of the woman, and so forth. So I'd say this tale falls under the category of "urban legend."

One story that *has* been substantiated, however, is that of a Georgia woman named Angela Cavallo, whose son had a near-miss on Good Friday in 1982. This incident was recounted in January 2006 by Cecil Adams, who is best known for his newspaper and Internet column, *The Straight Dope*. Adams reports that he actually spoke on the phone to Mrs. Cavallo, whose harrowing ordeal was originally reported in an April 1982 Associated Press story. Mrs. Cavallo was in her late fifties when the incident occurred. Her son Tony, a teenager at the time, was working on his 1964 Chevy Impala. The car was jacked up, and Tony had removed a rear tire and was working on the rear suspension. Then disaster hit.

One of the neighbor kids ran to Mrs. Cavallo's door to tell her there had been an accident, and when she ran out she found her son pinned under the car. Apparently Tony had accidentally rocked the car off the jack while trying to loosen something that had gotten stuck. Now he was caught in one of the rear wheel wells. The car had not crushed the young man, but he was out cold, and he was trapped for sure. His mother was in a panic, as you can imagine.

Mrs. Cavallo hollered at the neighbor kid to go get help, and then grabbed the side of the car with both hands, pulling up with all her strength. According to the AP account, she raised the car about four inches. She later said she doubted it was that much, but she believes it *was* enough to take the pressure off. She also says she recalls nothing about the rescue, but the AP story said that two neighbors were able to reinsert the jack and drag Tony out. Mrs. Cavallo estimates that she kept the car propped up for five minutes, and even though she describes herself as "5-foot-8, large-framed and strong," she is certain that under normal circumstances she couldn't have picked the car up. But she *did* manage to do it, and her son was freed. He recovered just fine.

Angela Cavallo's story is really not all that unusual. Occasionally you'll read a news report about someone saving another person by lifting a vehicle or some other heavy object off that person. Sometimes people are able to access this amazing physical strength to save themselves.

> ## It doesn't take a crisis for us to tap into incredible power! We all have that ability.

In 1999, a hiker in New Mexico had the scary experience of having his leg trapped under a 500-pound boulder – and according to his partner, he was able to lift the rock off of himself. The point is that most of us have heard about, or perhaps even experienced, incidents where people seem to demonstrate incredible physical strength in a time of intense crisis. So even though that mother-saves-baby tale may be an urban legend, it is one that, like many urban legends, is rooted in truth.

Scientists tell us that in situations like this, when we perceive danger, our mind becomes extremely focused on the single task of survival. The resulting adrenaline rush through our body – that well-known fight-or-flight response – imparts a kind of supercharged focused alertness and superhuman strength.

Fortunately, it doesn't take a life-threatening crisis in order for us to achieve this extraordinary strength and focus. Some psychologists and spiritual teachers tell us that we have the ability to tap into a universal power that is inside all of us, and that if we do we can achieve great things that seem superhuman to ordinary people in ordinary situations.

People call this energy that we tap into by different names, depending upon their beliefs. Some say that it's God helping us in times of need. Others call it the universal consciousness.

Others say it's the inner self or the higher self. I don't care what you call it, but it exists – and when we tap into it, we can indeed achieve remarkable things. Tapping into this inner power allows us to become extremely focused on our *intention* of what we want to accomplish. Of course, intention is not enough; action is necessary too. However, once we have that focus, taking the appropriate action is easy and even effortless.

Not many people experience extreme situations like those I described above, but world-class athletes and world-class achievers in all areas of life understand the secret of the inner power I'm talking about, and they use it to focus their desires to achieve many things that ordinary people consider impossible.

> **World-class achievers use their inner power to focus their desires and achieve things that ordinary people consider impossible.**

In this chapter, I will show you how to develop the same level of focus on your own desires. We're talking about the level of focus that enables a world-class figure skater to win the gold medal; or a quarterback to go out and win in the last minutes of the last quarter of the Super Bowl, or an entrepreneur to implement a new idea that makes millions of dollars.

These feats may seem out of your reach right now, even as you read these words, but that's all about to change. By the end of this chapter you will understand much more about the phenomenon of focused desire. It's very important that you do so, and that's why it's Step 3 in my Formula For Becoming A Millionaire. You will learn how to achieve *super-focused desire* in order to bring about whatever you want.

Desire is not enough

When I speak about desire, most people think in general terms about things that they wish for – things like having lots of money, being able to travel wherever they want, and the like. Maybe they think more in terms of specific material items, such as a new car or a second home in a tropical location like Hawaii. Generally, however, their desires center around living a life of luxury, having money and having all the free time they desire to relax and enjoy life.

There's nothing intrinsically wrong with any of this. Now, I realize that for some people the desire for material stuff becomes an unhealthy obsession, and the acquisition of more *things* becomes a substitute for having a real life. In case I haven't made it clear before now, this book is for people who have their priorities in order and simply want to make their lives better.

Whenever I ask people who have vague dreams of wealth just *how* they plan to accomplish their dreams, most of them have no answer. In fact, they've never even thought about how they're going to achieve all those wonderful things. Some people just consider their desires to be nothing more than pipe dreams – things they may think about wistfully but have no real hope of ever achieving. They speak in terms of, "If I ever won the lottery…" but know there's little chance *that* will ever happen.

Others, however, say they want to be rich and seem to think there's a chance that might happen eventually, but they have no clear idea of what they're going to do to *get* those riches.

What they are missing is a roadmap telling them how to get from where they are to where they want to be.

> # Lots of people want to be rich, but are missing The Formula to tell them how to get from where they *are* to where they *want to be*.

Let's say you live in Seattle and you want to drive to San Francisco. Most people know that to do this, you must get on the main freeway on Interstate 5 and start heading south. If you don't know this, of course, you can easily find a map to show you the way. As you travel south, you will begin to see signs indicating that you're on Interstate 5 heading south. As you get closer and closer to California, you'll begin to see signs that tell you the direction and the distance to San Francisco. These signs are there for anyone to see. If you are capable of reading and following the signs, it's a pretty sure bet you can get from Seattle to San Francisco with no problem.

What if you live in a place called Right Here, Right Now, and you want to go to a place called the Land of the Wealthy – which is where a lot of people want to go? Where do you begin? Countless people wish they could be rich, but they have no idea how to get started. They don't even know which direction to turn to begin their journey. Moreover, unlike the individual who merely wishes to drive from Seattle to San Francisco, the person who longs for wealth can't simply pick up a map at the local convenience store. To make things more difficult, the road to riches is not marked with obvious signs to keep you going in the right direction.

That doesn't mean you can't get there. You absolutely can, and you do it in the same way that the mother who lifted the car off her teenage son did, the same way that the Olympic runner breaks a world record, and the same way that the entrepreneur goes from having nothing to having over a billion dollars in only a few years.

> ## The road to riches is not marked with obvious signs.
> ## But my Formula can show the way to your "destination."

You get to the Land of the Wealthy through *focusing your desire*, knowing exactly what you want and what you're going to do to get from where you are now to where you want to be.

Equally as important, you accomplish it by *refusing to be distracted by:*

✦ your past failures

✦ the fact that you have nothing to show for all your life's hard work

✦ the busyness of your life

✦ the mundane chores that need to be tended to

✦ the fact that you have no money

✦ the people around you who say that you will never be successful.

Sometimes it seems incredibly difficult to filter out these distractions – particularly that last item, people who don't believe you can become successful – but you absolutely must do so in order to focus your desires.

Focus comes from within yourself when you learn to tap into that thing inside of you that's bigger than you are. That's what all of the great athletes do, and that's what the great entrepreneurs who are wealthy individuals do. By the time you're finished with this book you'll know exactly how to do that same thing – how to tap inside yourself to develop a clear, conscious and extraordinarily focused desire.

The Law Of Attraction

What I'm really talking about is the Law Of Attraction. How do you *attract* those things into your life that you want to have happen? If you want to be wealthy, for example, how do you attract money into your life? You have to create the level of desire for money that will allow you to focus on bringing it into your life. But how do you do that? And then how do you do what it takes to actually cause these things to come to you?

As I mentioned in the Introduction, the concept of the Law Of Attraction has been popularized in recent years. Writers such as Jerry and Esther Hicks have written about this topic in some of their books, and Australian producer Rhonda Byrne created a DVD and book called *The Secret*, which has become a phenomenal worldwide success. Even if you are not a fan of Jerry and Esther Hicks or of *The Secret*, I have found all of these works to contain some very useful truths about attracting what you want in life. You don't have to believe in the reality of the Hicks' information source, "Abraham," you don't have to be a fan of Rhonda Byrne or the teachers she chose for *The Secret*, and you don't even have to believe that the Law Of Attraction is a scientific law akin to gravity, in order to benefit from these truths.

You do, however, have to suspend your disbelief enough to work The Formula I am sharing in this book.

Many people think they understand the Law of Attraction, but the reality is that most people don't fully understand how to take advantage of it in their lives to bring about the results they want. That's because most of the hype around these topics encourages you to focus on what you can have, but it fails to tell you *what you must do in order to get it*.

Popular teachings on this subject suggest that when you create a belief within yourself and meditate on your desired outcome, you set into motion the things that are necessary to bring it about. Even more interesting is the suggestion that by meditating on *exactly what you want,* you set into motion the precise things in the universe to attract it.

I believe this is true, but it is only part of The Formula. That's why so many people try to practice The Law of Attraction, but still don't find success. The purpose of this book is to give you the *whole* Formula in seven simple and easy-to-follow steps.

We've already discussed Steps 1 and 2, which have to do with how you think and feel about money. Steps 3, 4, 5, 6 and 7 are the keys to unlocking the potential within you – and, yes, within the universe. And again, whether you are comfortable thinking in terms of the universe, or God, or Source, or whatever, it doesn't matter: the principles *work.* These principles have been and are used by athletes, billionaires and many of the greatest achievers who have ever walked this planet. All of these people have utilized these principles in one way or another, even if they weren't all consciously aware that they were doing so.

> # Popular teachings on the Law Of Attraction only cover part of The Formula. I give you a more complete picture by sharing *all* of the principles.

As I mentioned previously, I have studied the principles of wealth and success my whole life. I have worked with hundreds of wealthy individuals, investors and entrepreneurs, and I've helped them over the last twenty years to develop and accumulate wealth in their life. I've analyzed these principles, have figured out what works best and have organized the "cream of the crop" into this seven-part Formula, which you can understand and use right now to change your life.

Of course, I have applied these principles myself and have seen incredible – even borderline-miraculous – results in my own life. I can tell you from experience that by using my Formula, you don't have to wait around hoping that the universe will bring you what you want. This Formula will enable you to go out and *get* what you want.

You are the co-creator, along with the universe, of your life. It's up to you to make those things that you desire to have in your life a reality. And, yes, I do believe in being specific. If you want to have $100,000, using this Formula will guarantee that you will have $100,000. If you want $10 million, this Formula will guarantee that you have $10 million – but only if you use The Formula completely and are willing to follow through with what it requires of you in exchange for that $10 million.

Some people believe that success is part chance and part hard work. *I'm here to say chance has nothing to do with it; it is always 100% in your control.* You may not have 100% control over *all* of the events in your life or in the lives of those around you, but your success, or lack thereof, *is* 100% in your hands. I realize that even this statement is somewhat controversial. The idea of "100% responsibility" about anything sometimes translates into a blame game, where people are made to feel somehow guilty for misfortunes such as illness or natural disasters. That's not what my Formula is about at all. I'm certainly not here to lay any guilt on you. What I *am* here to do is help you claim the awesome power you may not have known you possess.

> ## My Formula shows how to think and act in ways to attract exactly what you want.

What prevents many people from realizing true success is that they don't understand the rules of the game. They don't understand how their own actions and thoughts either bring about the success they want or stop that success cold.

I'll teach you how to think and act in ways to attract exactly what you want. Whether it's money, career success, a wonderful relationship, good health, happiness or freedom, it's always up to you – and I maintain that it's always totally in your control. I emphasize, however, that it also always takes action on your part to bring about whatever it is that you want.

If you want money, you need to take action to get money. The good news is that once you begin developing the habit of using my Formula on a regular and consistent basis, then there are times when your thoughts alone appear to have the power to bring about exactly what you want.

My "everyday miracle"

Let me demonstrate by sharing a story of something that happened to me just a few months ago. I gave you an abbreviated version of this story in the Introduction to this book, but I'll give you the details now.

I was in the process of selling out my share of a multi-million dollar corporation that I owned with several other business partners. My share of the company was, by my calculation, worth approximately $1 million.

Understand that these were partners with whom I'd been in business for over fifteen years. I was good friends with them, and we had an excellent working relationship. However, during the course of negotiating the exact worth of my part of the company, we ran into a little bit of confusion regarding one line item that amounted to approximately $50,000. There seemed to be no clear consensus on whether or not I should be compensated for this amount.

In my mind, it was crystal clear that the fair thing to do was to pay me for that portion, but I knew some of my partners didn't necessarily agree. One night while I was home I began to contemplate the matter, and it wasn't long before I'd worked myself into an emotional state.

I started to really worry that I wasn't going to get the $50,000, and before I knew it I had worked myself into a state of righteous indignation, for I felt I was being cheated out of something that rightfully belonged to me. I began to get really angry, and began playing out a scenario in my head, going over what I would say to my partners, and the things they would say to me, and so forth. For about an hour, I had this purely hypothetical argument between my business partners and me.

> **The awesome power of The Formula is that if you follow it, everyone is successful and no one is slighted.**

My heart rate was going up, my face was turning red and I was becoming extremely frustrated and upset with my business partners. I wasn't chewing myself up over something that had happened, but something that I had entirely made up in my head. I bet you've done similar things yourself. It's easy to get all worked up over something that hasn't happened, isn't it?

Finally, after about an hour of becoming increasingly stressed and agitated, I caught myself and recognized what I was doing.

I recognized that I was not practicing or trusting in The Formula, because following The Formula will always bring about success in your life. Following The Formula will always make you feel happy, free and relaxed about what you're doing. It will always guarantee success – whether it's financial success or whatever other kind of success you want in your life.

I caught myself, I stopped myself and I began to focus on The Formula. I began to release, to let go, to trust that the universe, or God, or the ultimate consciousness – whatever you want to call it – was going to take care of me.

I began to put my faith and trust in something bigger than myself. I began to remember the seven principles I am sharing with you in this book. I immediately felt the stress go away from my body. I felt relaxed, I felt comfortable and, most of all, *I knew that everything was going to be okay.*

I remembered the first two principles, "Stop loving money," and "Realize money is just an idea." I focused my desires on what I truly wanted. I imagined some possibilities of how financially everything would work out. I imagined that I was going to *let go of this $50,000.* If my partners were not willing to give me this money, well, so what? I was going to accept that decision and I wasn't going to fight it, because I didn't want to ruin the relationships. They were worth far more to me than a mere $50,000.

I also made a deal with the universe/Source and said, "I trust that I will be taken care of financially, and if I lose this $50,000 right now, I trust that the universe is going to pay me back ten times that much money at some time in the near future." These were not just empty words. I truly felt confident and relaxed, and I felt a genuine sense of relief and joy from knowing that everything was really going to work out fine for all of us. (The process of imagining – and really feeling – the possibilities is the topic of the next chapter.)

Within two days, I got an email from the business manager who was putting together the final numbers. I carefully reviewed all the numbers. And did they include the $50,000 I was worried about? You bet they did.

I had spent so much time developing stress, creating arguments in my head and worrying about this $50,000, but the moment that I decided to stop and implement The Formula, things immediately got better. Not only did I feel better that evening and for the next couple of days while I was waiting for the attorneys and accountants to finish up their part, but everything really did work out. I've found this to be the case whenever I use The Formula. Miracles just seem to show up in my life.

But that's not the end of this story; there's still more. When I sold my interest in my company, not only did things work out well, they worked out considerably better than I had expected. Here's where the "miracle" part comes in, as far as I'm concerned. Reviewing the final numbers that the business manager had sent me, I looked at the bottom of the page – the part containing the summary telling me how much money was going to be paid to me. To my amazement, *it was $400,000 more than I had anticipated.*

Clearly, somebody had made a mistake. I was the CEO of that company, I knew what the numbers were supposed to be, I knew all of these line item numbers – and yet, according to the summary, I was about to be paid $400,000 more than I was owed. It had to be an error.

I got on the phone with the business manager and said, "Look, I've reviewed the numbers – everything looks great, everything's right on track as I expected – even that $50,000 that was in dispute. But you made an error in the summary; it's $400,000 too much. It must be a typo or something."

He replied, "No, Paul, we've reviewed the numbers. We've met with the attorneys, met with the accountants – we've been scrutinizing the numbers for the last several weeks, and that is the amount of money due to you."

> # Whenever I use The Formula, miracles just seem to show up in my life!

I thought, *"Wow, isn't that amazing.* Here I was two days ago, worrying about $50,000 – and then I caught myself and began to practice The Formula – and two days later, not only did I get my $50,000, but more miraculous than that, I got an extra $400,000."

Now, do you remember the deal I'd made with the universe two days prior to that? I had said, "I'm going to put this in your hands. I'm going to trust you and I'm going to trust that if I don't get the $50,000 you're going to make it up to me with ten times that much money." And then there I was two days later – and I got the $50,000 plus eight times that much money!

I'm not suggesting that things of this scale happen every day of my life, because they don't. But what I've found out is that when I practice this Formula consistently in my life, miracles like that do show up. And the more I practice The Formula, the more often they seem to show up. Coincidence? Dumb luck?

I don't think so!

So how do you learn to focus your desire in order for "everyday miracles" to show up in your own life?

The power of emotion

Let's talk some more about what desire is. Most people do a lot of wishing and wanting, but their desires are scattered all over the place. They want a lot of different things in their life. They want to be rich. They want to have more free time. They want a new car. They want a house. They want to remove all the stress in their life.

I like to ask them, "What do you want to happen first? What is it that you want to happen today that will move you closer to having what you want?" More often than not, they'll say, "Well, gee... I don't know." I ask them, "What is it that you want to happen this week that will move you in the direction of having what you want?" They say, "Well, I don't know... maybe win the lottery?"

> ## You want to be a millionaire,
> ## but do you have a plan?
> ## So does everyone else.
> ## But the wealthy
> ## use The Formula
> ## for becoming a millionaire.

That's not good enough – not nearly good enough.

I ask, "What are you doing about it today – or even this month – that will move you towards your desire?" And almost all of them reply, "Well, I'm not doing anything." I say, "What have you done in the last year to move you in the direction that you want – the direction that will change your financial situation and make you become a millionaire?" If they're honest, most of them will say, "Nothing. I've done nothing that will make me a millionaire."

As you've no doubt figured out, I can be pretty persistent when I have these conversations with people. I say, "Well, do you have plans during the next twelve months? What are you going to do to make yourself become a millionaire, since you say that's what you want to become?" They say (you guessed it), "I don't have a plan."

Where there's no plan, there's no focus – and I can guarantee you that there will be no millionaire.

I can pretty much guarantee that you will not become a millionaire if you don't have a clear desire for what you want to have happen in your life, and a focused plan for next week, next month and through this next year.

In a future chapter, we'll talk about how to create your action plan. For now, we'll concentrate on how to focus your desire. Whether it's money or a great relationship or a new home – whatever it is – the way to focus your desire is to mix that desire with positive emotions.

Once you decide what you want to have happen in your life – what you want to have happen today, this week and next month – you have taken the first step towards focused desire. Then you must create a positive emotion that goes along with your desires. You have the potential to create either positive or negative emotions. So how do you create positive emotions that align with the desires that you want? I'm going to tell you how to do that.

It's a crucial skill to learn, because once you create a positive emotion that goes along with your desire, it sets into motion an invisible energy within you that causes you to begin to notice the opportunities around you. It almost seems that the universe brings opportunities to you. You begin meeting people you need to meet. Money starts coming into your life, sometimes from unexpected sources. You get phone calls from people who can help you create a product or service you've envisioned. Whatever it is that you're trying to do in your life to get wealthy, when you begin to have a clearly focused desire for what you want to have happen – and you mix it with positive emotions – things begin to fall into place in your life.

> # Mixing focused desire with positive emotions, sets an invisible energy into motion.

Let me give you an example of an everyday situation in which you have an emotional reaction that could be either positive or negative, depending upon what you choose to feel. Let's say that you're walking down a city sidewalk early one evening and you see a limousine pull up in front of a fancy hotel. Out steps a beautiful woman dressed in an elegant gown and wearing diamonds. She's ready to go to a ball or a fancy dinner. Beside her is a man with a tuxedo. He has a dark tan that he probably got when he was out on the golf course at a resort in Maui a couple of days ago. You can imagine that they probably just flew in on their private jet. As the limousine pulls away, the couple is escorted into the ballroom of this grand hotel. As you watch them, you develop an emotional response, because you want to have the wealth that they have. You are either going to create a positive emotion or a negative emotion.

If you create a positive emotion around what you're watching, you're going to say, "I'm happy for them, because they have figured out how to be successful. They have figured out how to create wealth in their life, and they're living the lifestyle that I would love to live. In fact, they're living the lifestyle that I'm going to be living in the very near future!"

You have developed a very positive emotional response to what you have just witnessed. And that's a good thing; it is precisely the kind of emotional response you need to create every single day, many times a day. That is perfectly in sync with your desire to be wealthy.

Many people, on the other hand, create a negative emotional response. When they see rich people, they think, "Why do they get to be rich and I can't? I don't know if I'm ever going to be rich... I can't even pay my bills." Maybe you are a little bit envious, seeing those fancy clothes, that sleek limousine, those enviable tans from their last vacation. And you think, "I'm never going to have that. Life doesn't seem fair – why do they get to have all that and I don't?"

Negative emotions prevent you from seeing the opportunities in front of you.

You may even have a sour-grapes response, thinking in terms of the "miserable rich" stereotype we see so often on television. Or you might get on your moral high horse and condemn the couple for being greedy and selfish and wasteful of resources.

These are all negative emotions, and when you create those negative emotions, you aren't hurting the rich couple at all; you are doing nothing but sabotaging your own life and happiness. Creating negative emotions like this guarantees that you are not going to have the wealth they have because your subconscious is sending forth energy that is going to stop you from seeing the opportunities in front of you.

In fact, you're going to start noticing the obstacles all around you – and it's going to appear almost as if the universe is bringing you obstacles rather than opportunities.

If you can learn to create positive emotions within yourself – and mix them with the focused desire of what you want, and what you're going to do to become wealthy –then you have taken the first steps to creating the energy within yourself that's going to make you a millionaire.

Focused desire starts with you thinking about what you want. Oftentimes, it's triggered by what you see around you, what other people are doing. When you create a positive emotion within yourself and mix it with your focused desire to be wealthy, you set into motion that invisible energy I mentioned earlier. It allows you to see the opportunities all around you, and you can pull yourself closer to the financial success that you desire.

When you do this, opportunities just seem to come your way. It's almost as if someone or something is on your side, clearing the path for you to become successful. Desire starts within you when you begin to think clearly about what you want today, next week, next month and next year. Many times your desires are triggered when you see other people's success.

Desire is both triggered and reinforced by what you see and by what you talk about. You see celebrities on TV, you see their riches and their fame, and you can either be consumed with envy or moral outrage, or you can say, "Hey, that's the lifestyle I want to live." (Okay, so maybe you don't want to be one of those out-of-control party girls – or boys – who are always making the tabloid headlines, but there are certain trappings of the good life that are well worth pursuing, in my opinion.) The point is that looking at the example of other people's lives allows you to form mental imprints of things that you desire to have. That's the beginning – but you have to mix it with the emotional response, the positive emotions that I just described.

Desire starts within you when you begin to think clearly about what you want today, next week, next month and next year.

The positive emotions are like the adrenaline rush that an athlete has when he's in position on the starting line, ready to hear the starting gun for the beginning of an Olympic race. It's like the mother grabbing the bumper of the car, lifting it with all her strength to raise the vehicle off her child.

It's like the adrenaline of an entrepreneur who has just found a piece of real estate he believes will make him $10 million richer – and he's just about ready to go into a meeting with the seller of that property to begin negotiating a sale price. (This is a rush I can testify to firsthand.)

It's like the adrenaline of a figure skater who has dreamed of going to the Olympics ever since she was five years old. Every day of her life for the last twelve years, she has spent five or six hours training and practicing for this performance – and now she's about to go out onto the ice for her final performance. The adrenaline is rushing, but she is prepared – she's ready and she knows that this is the moment in which victory is sure to be hers.

That's the type of emotion that winners learn to create within themselves each time they think about what they want – and especially when they focus on what they're going to do to ensure their success. When you mix positive emotion as I just described with a focused desire on what you want, you are well on your way to achieving greatness.

Earlier I said that you are the co-creator of your life, along with the universe. That means you have an incredibly powerful ally, so why not make the most of that alliance? I am not for a moment suggesting that you are omnipotent and that every-thing around you is completely under your control. But you *do* have control over much more than you might have previously imagined. And whether you choose to think in terms of God, or Source, or a marvelously responsive universe, you can use the powers within you to create an unhappy life... or a mediocre life... or an extraordinary life.

It's up to you.

Now come with me while we take a closer look at the art of imagining possibilities – that's Step 4 in my Formula For Becoming A Millionaire. This is where the journey really gets exciting.

**Greatness
is achieved only through
focusing your mind
on exactly what you want,
and not letting
anything distract you.**

*Nothing can come into being
without first being imagined.*

*More valuable than intelligence
or education or knowledge,
imagination is
the beginning of everything,
and the secret key
that will unlock the door
to endless possibilities
in your life.*

STEP 4

IMAGINE And FEEL The Possibilities

This is Step 4 in my seven-part Formula For Becoming A Millionaire: IMAGINE ~ AND FEEL ~ THE POSSIBILITIES. Among other things you will learn:

1. *The simple secret to wealth that 96% of the world's population refuses to accept*
2. *The one thing that everyone has that trumps skill, smarts and luck as a tool for creating a life of wealth and freedom*

So far in this book, we have discussed the necessity of changing your thinking about money and wealth if you want to become a millionaire. We've tackled some of the most counterproductive – and downright destructive – misconceptions that keep all too many people locked in "poverty consciousness" and therefore in a perpetual cycle of hard work and financial distress. We've covered the importance of focusing your desires, and tapping into a power greater than yourself, in order to create a lifestyle of wealth and abundance.

That's a lot of ground to cover in three chapters. Well, hold on; we're just getting warmed up.

In this chapter, we will go beyond the subject of desire and into the realm of imagination. This isn't a frivolous exercise; *imagination is one of your most powerful tools for wealth building.* And *imagination fueled by emotion is perhaps the most powerful tool of all.* In the previous chapter we talked about the influence of emotions, but we are going to approach that subject from a slightly different, but related, angle in this chapter.

Do you STILL believe those lies?

What if you had no money but I showed you how to create money by using your imagination? What if you had no way to afford a new car, but I showed you how to get a brand new BMW without spending a dime of your own money and without getting into debt – all by using your imagination?

What if I could show you how to become a real estate entrepreneur, owning millions of dollars in real estate – and how to do it without having any money – having little more than your imagination?

At this point, even though you've come this far on the journey with me, you still might be scoffing at the idea that imagination can be so powerful. Your skepticism is understandable, given the money myths that most of us were taught from childhood. That's why I spent the first couple of chapters of this book trying to rid you of those destructive beliefs. And that's why I'm going to continue that process here, because I know how deeply ingrained these beliefs are, and I know you still might not be entirely convinced that they are blatant falsehoods that will do nothing but keep you from ever being wealthy. So even though I've said it before, I'm going to say it again:

1. Working hard *has nothing to do with building wealth.*
2. Having a job *has nothing to do with building wealth.*
3. Being smart *has nothing to do with building wealth.*
4. Having the "right" education *has nothing to do with building wealth.*

5. Knowing the "right" people *has nothing to do with building wealth*.

Or you can turn it around and say:

To build incredible amounts of wealth, *even when you're beginning with no money at all...*

1. You don't have to work hard.
2. You don't have to have a job.
3. You don't have to be smart.
4. You don't have to have the "right" education.
5. You don't have to know the "right" people.

Sure, some of these factors can give you an advantage in some aspects of your life. (And *meeting* the right people can certainly be helpful once you're on the road to building your wealth.) However, the things I listed above simply are not essential ingredients in my Formula For Becoming A Millionaire. In particular, having a job – where you spend most of your waking hours working for someone else for a limited amount of pay – is one factor that is almost guaranteed to keep you from *ever* realizing the kind of wealth we're talking about.

What would you say if I told you that building massive amounts of wealth has more to do with your imagination than with anything else?

> # Building massive amounts of wealth has more to do with YOUR IMAGINATION than with anything else.

It's true.

It's also very good news, because imagination is free, and everyone has it. Imagination is the basic ingredient that makes four percent of the wealthiest people in the world different from everyone else. The people in this small but very wealthy minority are willing to believe something so outrageously simple that most people dismiss it as being simply too good to be true.

The vast majority of people believe that wealth must be difficult to acquire, and that it must require a lot of hard work and great intelligence. That's why most people are working themselves to death – having no time to play, no extra money and no fun – while wondering why they aren't getting any richer. And that's why so many just give up altogether, believing that they "don't have a head for business" or that they just don't have the level of intelligence necessary to make the big money.

Only a few people dare to believe the simple truth I'm about to tell you – and these are the people who are lying on the beaches on Maui or Tahiti or Malibu, making more money while they're having fun than they ever made when they were toiling away at the daily grind. They are accumulating wealth as they sleep, as they play and as they do whatever they take pleasure in doing. It is these few people who understand the secret I'm about to tell you – the secret contained in Step 4.

Einstein understood this secret when he said, "Imagination is more important than knowledge." Of course Einstein didn't spend a life of luxury sunbathing on Maui, but he did change the face of physics, altering the way we viewed reality and causing us to question many long-held assumptions. More important to my point, *he understood the incredible power of imagination.*
It is a power that can turn the world upside down. It is a power that can turn lives around. It is a power that can transform a person who has nearly nothing into a millionaire or a billionaire. And yet so many of us fail to take advantage of this enormous power we all possess.

Imagination is the beginning of everything

Let's say you want to create mass amounts of wealth, perhaps through growing your business or your income 1,000 times larger than what it is right now. Or perhaps you've had a vision about something you want to accomplish in this world, and you want to expand that vision a thousand-fold. Well, there's only one way to do that. There's only one way to make something grow 1,000 times – or more – bigger than it is right now.

There are a lot of ways *not* to do it. You can't work 1,000 times longer or 1,000 times smarter or 1,000 times harder. You cannot tell the world to pay you 1,000 times more money than whatever the world is paying you right now for doing whatever it is you do. (Okay...technically you could *tell* the world to increase your pay 1,000 times, but I can almost guarantee that you would be disappointed in the results.)

However, you *can* imagine 1,000 times bigger. Imagination is free, and you can do whatever you want with it.

If you want to figure out a way to double your salary by imagining some way of doing it, you can do that – but just as easily you can imagine your salary going up ten, a hundred, one thousand times or even more. Imagination is free, no matter how big the vision is. That's what this chapter is about: imagining the possibilities.

Imagination is the beginning of everything. All things that are created in the world – manmade or otherwise – had to have their beginning in someone's imagination. All wealth at first had to be imagined in the mind of the person who created it. All the billionaires in the world had to at first imagine what they were going to do to become a billionaire. *Their imaginings were not necessarily focused upon the billions of dollars, but rather on expanding the scope of their passion beyond its current limits.*

Imagination is the beginning of everything. All the billionaires in the world had to first imagine what they were going to do to become a billionaire.

Whatever their passion was – whether it was the creation of wealth and money itself or whether it was something else that captured their interest – they began with their imaginations.

Look at all the products around you – everything you buy for your home: chairs, tables, couches, furniture, computers, printers, cell phones, iPods... all of these things first had to be imagined before they existed.

That's easy enough to understand, right? Every manufactured product you see had its humble beginnings in someone's imagination before it came into existence. Eventually, that person or persons imagined ways to turn their vision into a reality – in other words, they found a way to bring value to you. So in a very real sense, you have furniture, computers, printers, telephones and all these other products that you now use because someone used his or her imagination.

The same goes with all of the services we purchase. When we go out to eat, we have people wait on us and bring us food. Broadcast services, cable companies or satellite TV companies provide us with television. Our Internet access is brought to us by a service provider as well. All of those services all had to be imagined before they were created.

Many of the companies that bring us products or services are huge nationwide or worldwide organizations that may seem impersonal. Thus it's easy to forget that they were first imagined into existence by people who perhaps aren't all that different from you and me. Each and every product or service these massive companies provide *had its origins in somebody's imagination.* Whether that imagination belonged to one individual or a couple of people or a small group of entrepreneurs or an entire department within the company, none of these products or services would exist if some person or persons had not first imagined them.

Imagination turns to Belief. Belief turns to Action. Action creates whatever you desire.

You too have the potential to create your own multi-million dollar product or service or whatever you want to do – and my hope is that it's something that you're passionate about (we'll discuss passions some more later on in this chapter). But it all starts with imagination.

It wasn't so long ago that horseless carriages and flying machines didn't exist outside the imaginations of a few visionaries. And not so long ago, going to the moon was the stuff of H.G. Wells novels, but few ordinary people seriously thought that humans would really be able to make that journey. It wasn't all that long ago that robots were imaginary, and now they are used everywhere: in manufacturing, surgery and even household cleaning. Computers were imaginary not too long ago as well, and even for many years after their invention, they were behemoths that took up entire buildings. The thought of a powerful personal computer that could fit on someone's desktop wasn't even conceivable to the average person until a few young entrepreneurs came along in the 1970s.

Everything that *Is* had to first be *Imagined.*

I remember when I was a kid watching *The Jetsons* on TV. Besides robots and all of those other futuristic devices, the Jetsons had flat-panel TV monitors. Even at that time, having such a thing as a flat panel TV monitor or computer monitor was only imaginary. On *The Jetsons*, people talked to each other over the flat-panel computer monitor the way we talked on a telephone, but even when I was a child that was an object that existed only in someone's imagination. Today, it's a reality. Not everybody uses this technology (yet), but it's clearly a reality, and people all over the world *are* using it to communicate with one another.

Another device seen on *The Jetsons* and in numerous science-fiction movies and books is the flying car. For many years, that was purely imaginary, and although the flying car is not at all commonplace nowadays, we hear about them, read about them and know they exist. We know people have them, they're testing them and they play with them. They are not used by ordinary drivers – and some people doubt they will be or even *should* be any time soon – but they are used for toys by some wealthy people, and one inventor is testing a model that may be for sale within the next few years. The point is that, folly or not, flying cars exist, whereas a few decades ago only the imaginary cartoon character George Jetson had one.

Although it took decades for the flying car to become a reality, you and I don't have to wait that long to create our own wonders. We are capable right now of imagining things we can create next month, next year and even into the next three years. You can easily imagine what you want to be doing in your life three years from now. You can be a millionaire, quit your day job, be playing on the beaches of Hawaii, living a life of luxury – not forty years in the future, but a mere three years from now – *if* you follow the principles in my Formula For Becoming A Millionaire.

And the first thing I want you to do, now that you've cleared your thinking of all of those myths and misconceptions that are keeping you poor, is to…

IMAGINE THE POSSIBILITIES!

"How long till I get rich, Paul?"

When I teach classes about my Formula For Becoming A Millionaire, people ply me with questions. Some of the most common ones are:

1. How long until I make my first million dollars if I do everything you teach me?
2. If I put your Formula into practice, how long is it going to take me to get rich?
3. How long is it going to take before I can quit my job and be independently wealthy?

These are all understandable questions, of course, but there is no way I can give a reasonable answer to any of them without asking some more questions of my own. The short answer is: "It's all up to you." That's not a cop-out. When I talk to someone about deciding their own path to wealth, one of the things I insist we talk about first is deciding exactly what that person wants. More importantly, what is the path *they* want to take to get rich? After all, there are as many ways to get rich as there are rich people – maybe even more.

> **You CAN
> generate wealth automatically,
> doing what
> you love to do.**

Frequently, my question just prompts the person to ask *me* another question. People say to me, "I don't know, Paul – what's the best way to get rich?" In fact, "What's the best way to get rich?" is another one of the questions I receive most frequently.

People ask, "Should I try to get rich in real estate? Should I do it in the stock market? Should I just keep buying lottery tickets and use that Law Of Attraction thing to get the odds more in my favor?"

Most people realize that many ways of getting rich do take some work, and some of those ways take hard work. On the other hand, that old standby, the lottery, takes hardly any work at all – just luck. Yet the odds are so astronomically *against* winning big in any lottery that it's just not a method I could in good conscience recommend. Still, most people want to know if there is an easy, or at least an easi*er*, way to get rich. "Isn't there some secret that can bring me wealth automatically without my having to work myself to death? Is that even possible?" they ask me. And I reply, "Yes, it is possible, but only when you understand my entire Formula."

So again we come back to the questions every aspiring millionaire asks at one time or another: "How long till I make my first million?" "When can I tell my boss to take this job and shove it?" "What's the best way to get rich?"

And again I say, "It's up to you." Whatever you do, though, don't overlook the amazing tool that resides inside you all the time: your imagination.

How long will it be before you make your first million? It's ALL up to you!

Turn thorns into roses!

On the road to wealth, you will almost certainly encounter people in your life who will slow you down. Some may try, in ways both subtle and blatant, to keep you from getting where you want to go. They may tell you that what you desire is impossible. They may say, "Stop wasting your time daydreaming and imagining you're going to be rich." They'll insist that those visions of beaches on Maui or villas in Tuscany are not for you but only for the lucky few – the glamorous film stars, the business tycoons whose combination of shrewdness and greed made them wealthy, or the silver-spoon brigade who grew up on the "right side of the tracks." They'll say your dreams of wealth and freedom are not realistic, and they'll chide you for risking your steady job and stable life for the great unknown, that part of the map where, in their minds, "Beyond here there be dragons." In other words, you are almost sure to be faced with people who cling stubbornly to all of those false beliefs we talked about in earlier chapters.

Maybe you are already dealing with some of these folks.

I know exactly what you are going through, because at one time there were people in my life who opposed everything I did. They seemed to be slowing me down. I wanted them out of my way, but they were "stuck" in my life for various reasons. I couldn't get rid of them. They were a thorn in my side.

This might sound a little callous to you – unless you happen to have some of the same kind of people in *your* life. Don't get me wrong; I am not discounting anyone's value as a human being, and I honestly do believe we can learn valuable lessons from everyone in our life, but there are some people who really do seem determined to keep others down. These are the people for whom the expression, "Misery loves company" was invented. Many of us have been faced with people like this. If you have, you know how hard it can be to improve your own life when you are surrounded by their negative influence.

Surround yourself with people who think Wealth and Abundance thoughts if you want to BECOME WEALTHY.

If they are casual acquaintances, it may not be such a big problem to remove yourself from that influence. However, if the people who seem to want to keep you anchored in your rut are close coworkers or neighbors or, even worse, family members, getting away can be more of a challenge. Let's say you have a passive-aggressive office mate who makes snide little remarks whenever you mention something you're doing that you believe can make you wealthy. Or perhaps you have a sister-in-law who's stuck in a dead-end job and is hopelessly in debt; suppose she feels a need to call you every night complaining about how awful her life is. If you don't spend thirty minutes commiserating with her – or even worse (in her view), if you attempt to share some good news from *your* life – she does her best to make you feel guilty for being cold and unfeeling. And you can count on her to always be the loudest detractor, the first one to shoot down any idea you might have that could lead to a life of freedom and wealth.

Even people who are genuinely concerned for your well-being may hit you with this kind of negativity. Just keep in mind that their concerns are based in their own fears, and that their expressions are a statement of their own inability to imagine something more than they currently experience.

Still, the naysayers can be maddening to deal with. What is a person to do when faced with these kinds of people?

Well, believe it or not, this is yet another way you can use Step 4, *imagine the possibilities.* You can use this Formula to change the people in your life, to cause them either to get out of your life or change so they're no longer a thorn in your side.

> ## Just remember that every person has value, and everyone has something to teach you.

"Yeah, right, Paul," I hear you reply. "I'll just use my imagination to *imagine* a magic wand, then I'll pull it out of my… um…hat, and, POOF! The person who was giving me so much grief will just disappear into thin air – or they'll become my biggest cheerleader. Or maybe it would be quicker for me to just hop into my flying car and go find a hit man or something."

All right, all right. As I've said before, a little cynicism is understandable, especially since there are so many people out there promising seemingly magical solutions to every problem. But here's the deal: what I'm talking about can and does really work, and, yes, the results may at times seem magical or miraculous. Remember that story I shared in the previous chapter about the anguish I went through when selling my share of my company? Although much of my agony was the product of my imagination (and there's a *negative* use of imagination if I ever saw it!), the doubts I had about whether I would get my fair share of the money were based upon some real conflicts I had been having with some of my partners. When I made the choice to "let go" and let the universe/Source handle it – and when *I imagined a possibility* where everything worked out well for all of us – well, guess what? I got my "miracle."

> ## Imagine – and feel – the possibility that everything will work out for the best. Then it will become a reality.

That's why I suggest that when dealing with difficult people of any type, you *imagine a possibility* where you are becoming happier (and richer), and that person is actually happy for you – or at the very least, is no longer trying to stand in your way. Better yet, imagine *the best of all possibilities for that person.* Imagine him or her becoming rich and happy too! After all, the human imagination is boundless. Surely there's room for more than one person in at least some of your imaginings. (Besides, I know from experience that creating such pleasant visions about another person is a lot better for your blood pressure than all those fantasies of you throttling that person!)

I am not even going to try to explain how Step 4 works in these situations. I'm not going to hit you with any theories about physics or metaphysics, because those aren't my areas of expertise. Besides, some people might argue that just by making up your mind to change your thinking and *imagine the possibilities*, you're not actually changing the other person. You're merely changing your own behavior in a way that encourages the other person to react to you in ways that are more to your liking. Or maybe you're changing your *perceptions* so that you don't find the other person so objectionable anymore. Or perhaps you become clearer in your thinking and more courageous in your relationships, and thus you have the clarity and courage to finally sit down and have a good heart-to-heart with the person. Or maybe you find that as you learn to focus more on your own dreams, you begin feeling more hopeful and self-confident, to the point where the other person's opposition simply doesn't bother you nearly as much as it used to.

In some cases, it could even be that once you start looking more honestly and clearly at the situation, you see that maybe – just maybe – the person who's been giving you problems has some legitimate gripes after all. There's a small possibility, you concede, that at times you may have behaved a little bit like a horse's patoot, and that person is just calling you on it.

(**Use your AWESOME IMAGINATION to create some AWESOME REALITIES!**)

Depending upon the person and the situation, any or all of the above could be true. I won't discount any explanation. But if imagining the possibilities (and using the rest of my Formula) *works*, no matter how or why it works – why not do it? I should tell you, however, that I *have* seen conflict situations (apart from my own experience with the company sale) where "imagining the possibilities" seemed to work on more than just the person doing the imagining. These were situations where one person decided to "work The Formula," particularly Step 4, and the other person made a complete turnaround in their behavior – one that was noticeable to outside parties who didn't have a personal stake in the relationship. Of course, that's still anecdotal evidence rather than hard scientific proof, but it's pretty powerful evidence, as far as I'm concerned.

I've gone to some lengths here to discuss difficult people because they really can be a serious obstacle on the road to wealth. So many people fail to handle these problems as well as they could, and it's not because they are bad people or even because those who are giving them trouble are bad folks. In many cases it is simply because they do not know how to use their imagination to rise above the conflict and see the greater picture.

When you are on the road to creating your extraordinary life, other people you encounter can be either a help or a hindrance. You might be surprised at how easy it is to turn the latter into the former – with just a little imagination.

The universe can't do it alone

In the previous chapter I said you are the co-creator of your life, along with the universe/Source or whatever you want to call it. As I noted, that big Whatever can be a powerful ally, but if you just sit and wait for the universe to do it all, you'll be waiting in perpetuity. Remember that the other factor in this great equation is *you*, and your most powerful and versatile tool is that imagination of yours.

There really is no limit to what you can create with your imagination, and we're not just talking about money. We're not just talking about creating wealth. We're talking about creating *a whole person* who is not only wealthy, but also happy and healthy. We're talking about a person who has all the free time desired to enjoy every aspect of life.

And that profound change begins with imagination.

It is so simple, yet as I said earlier, it's precisely because it's so simple that most people fail to believe in it. So I'm asking you to dare to believe in the power of your imagination to change your life incredibly – making you richer and happier and freer than you've ever dreamed possible.

> **There really is no limit to what you can create with your imagination...
> not just money, but *a whole person* who is wealthy, happy and healthy.**

Do you know people for whom it seems that everything goes right? They always seem to be at the right place at the right time. They meet the right people and great things happen to them. Every enterprise of theirs prospers. They make money. If they have a job, they get promotions, the boss likes them, and they seem to move up the corporate ladder very fast.

Yet here *you* are working away at the same position year after year. The boss barely knows you're alive, and the last time you got a promotion or a raise was…well, never!

Then along comes this new person from nowhere – with no experience, younger than you, perhaps better-looking to boot (for those who like that type, anyway)… and they seem to climb the ladder and prosper. Everyone loves them, everything they touch turns to the proverbial gold, and they become a huge success. They're the new shining star in the company.

Why does that happen? Are they just lucky? Were they at the right place at the right time? Probably not. Provided they're not sleeping their way to the top, and not related to the top brass in some way, you can pretty much assume that they are so successful because they understand at least part of The Formula I'm sharing with you in this book.

Most significantly for this chapter, they understand *how to use imagination* to get where they want to go. They know that once you've unleashed the power of imagination, everything seems to fall into place. *That's* what those people have going for them.

This brings us back to the question: Why do so few people know the secret? Why do so few people get wealthy? Why is it that 96% of the people in the world are not rich? Why do only four percent of the people understand this secret, and because of that they're healthy, wealthy, happy, and *they* control the lion's share of the world's wealth?

It's very tempting to fall back on traditional thinking when trying to explain how this four percent got so wealthy. And it's really tempting not to believe imagination played a part in their wealth, and by extension not to believe in imagination at all – because you want something more concrete. You want me to tell you, "Here's what you do – go buy this stock. Here's what you do – you buy this particular real estate. Here's what you do – start a business and grow it like this." That's understandable, because those are very concrete things, and we like to believe in concrete things. We can see them, touch them, feel them… and, most importantly, we can watch them grow. Most of us also like to be given precise, step-by-step instructions. We like to have our hand held through a new or difficult process.

So when I talk about imagination, you might think I am skirting the issue. Yet even as I said that "Money is an idea, not an object," I also say that all your wealth has nothing to do with concrete physical things. It is more about how you think about yourself, and how you think about money – and all of *that* has to do with how you use your imagination to create in your mind what you want. That's where it all starts. It really has very little to do with the things you buy, or the activities in which you participate. It *does* have 90% to do with your thought processes about wealth and about yourself. Again, all of that has to do with how you use your imagination.

> **Wealth is not just about concrete physical things.**
> **It is more about how you think of yourself, and how you use your imagination to create what you want in your mind.**

People don't want to believe that, because it seems too simple or perhaps too fanciful. So not many people *do* believe it, and that's why not many people are wealthy. The good news for you is that it *is* so simple, and it's free, and there are no pre-requisites. You don't have to have any college education, you don't have to be smart and you don't have to work hard.

All you have to do is use your imagination to create what you want in your life. There's an entire universe out there that's willing to help fulfill those desires – but the universe can't do it without you.

"Enough with the theories, Paul; give me some real examples!"

How do you use imagination to create what you want in your life? So many people ask me, "Where do I start, Paul? I know I have to figure out a way to create wealth, but I'm not sure just how I want to do it. Do you have any ideas for me?"

Well, as I said earlier, "It's up to you." I can't make that decision for you! The best way to create wealth is by doing whatever it is that you absolutely love to do in your life.

Plato said that necessity is the mother of invention, but if that is so, passion must surely be the father. Many people have built huge business empires around things they were particularly passionate about. In a little while I'll share a story of some folks who have done just that.

> **Plato said that necessity is the mother of invention. Passion must surely be the father.**

I know you've heard the term, "Do what you love, and the money will follow." There's even a book by that title. Actually, though, that concept is a bit misleading. Just doing what you love won't guarantee that you get rich – unless you are working The Formula For Becoming A Millionaire at the same time. However, doing what you love will make becoming a millionaire *fun* – and almost effortless. It will also make it much easier for you to reinforce your imagination with positive emotion. And as I've said before, imagination fueled by emotion is one of the most powerful forces in creation.

That's why I strongly encourage people who are looking for their own pathway to wealth to first look to the things that interest them most.

I was in Seattle a few months ago at an expo. I had a display at a trade booth and a woman came up to me, and we got into a conversation about her desires to become wealthy. She asked the classic question: "But Paul, what can *I* do to become rich?" I answered this old favorite with my own favorite question. I said, "What is it you love to do?"

She laughed and said, "Well, nothing... the only thing I really love to do is karaoke. But obviously, that's not going to make me a lot of money!"

I said, "What do you mean? Of *course* it can make you a lot of money!" She looked at me, puzzled but hopeful.

I continued, "How big is karaoke? A lot of people love karaoke. It's all over the country. It's in every state, every city, it's in nearly ever major metropolitan area. People love karaoke. It's even big in other countries besides Japan!"

I was really getting warmed up now. I said, "Look, when there are lots of people who love something you also love – then there's an opportunity! So the question becomes, how can you use your imagination to create for yourself a way to build wealth *and* bring value to other people through something you – and they – love?"

She replied, "Well, I love to teach other people… and I've helped other people get started. I've helped them learn how to do the sound systems. I know nearly everything there is to know about karaoke."

Now she was really getting enthusiastic. "I work as a manager at this restaurant where we have karaoke," she explained. "I could train, mentor and teach people how to get started, set it up… even form businesses doing karaoke. In fact, I really like helping people. I like to coach people and get them started. I like to give them encouragement."

"That is amazing," I replied. "And it's exactly what I'm talking about. So what's the best way you could reach millions of people?"

She seemed at a loss for an answer, so I continued, "Instead of doing one-on-one coaching, you could do things like hold classes over the Internet. And of course you could write books."

She replied, "I never thought of that. I love writing! And you know, that would actually work. Believe it or not, millions of people would buy that book. I know they would, because I'm in the business."

I said, "See, there you go. The key is imagination – it just takes a little spark to get you thinking about how you can take something you love, even something that you initially think can't make money, like karaoke."

How about you? How can you imagine ways that you can bring great value to the world in ways where millions of people would pay millions of dollars to you to continue doing what it is you love to do?

> **How can you bring value to the world in ways that millions of people would pay you to continue doing what you love to do? Figure that out, and you're well on your way to being a (happy) millionaire!**

I happen to love horses; I ride horses and have several on my property. I know a lot of people who are into horses, but I also know that although they are among God's most glorious creatures, horses are also high-dollar, high-maintenance animals. You have to buy the horse, which can be expensive. They're expensive to feed, and you have to keep them stabled somewhere, which incurs a monthly cost if you don't have your own facilities. Training them can also be costly. If you show them or race them, it's possible to make a little money, but it's also expensive and it's not at all a sure thing. It can cost a pretty penny to keep them healthy too. As I said, they're high-maintenance!

For most people, horse ownership is a fairly expensive hobby to have, so most people don't see horses as a way to make money; rather, they see owning horses as something that *costs* a lot of money.

Well, suppose you really love horses, and that love keeps insinuating itself into your visions of wealth and happiness? You keep pushing it away, because, after all, you can't make money with horses.

Or can you? Well, I know a lot of people who give riding instructions to horse lovers. They have classes. They have stables. They board horses – and you can make a little money boarding horses if you have a big stable, but you'll never get rich from it.

You won't become wealthy. So what if you want to bring your equine friends along with you on the road to riches? What type of vision could you have?

Suppose someone came to me and said, "Paul, what I love most in my life is horses. I love to ride. I love being around horses. I love training horses. But there's just no way to make money with horses unless you're racing them – and even that is a huge gamble and risk. And I don't even have enough money to buy a horse for myself right now, to say nothing of getting rich using my love of horses."

Here is what I would say: *"Use your imagination.* Blow up your dream 1,000 times bigger than it is now."

Perhaps they would say, "Okay – I can imagine that I can get money to buy a horse and money to maintain the horse. And I can even imagine myself using your principles to get more money in order to buy my own ranch. I could have my own horses, board horses and give classes to people...."

I'd say, "Okay that's a start. But you know and I know you're not going to get rich doing that – so blow it up 1,000 times bigger."

How do you blow it up 1,000 times bigger? You do it with imagination. That's the only way to do it. And in case your imagination is still just plodding along at this point, maybe the story I'm about to share will serve as a good "Giddy-up!"

Can't think of a way to make money doing what you love to do?
Use your imagination!
Download my FREE Report
Top 10 Ways To Create Wealth
www.FormulaForMillionaires.com.

A few years ago, when I first started getting into horses, I took lessons from a woman I worked with. She taught me how to ride. One day she invited me out to a local fair, where a husband-and-wife team from Colorado were giving lessons in something called "natural horsemanship." Their names are Pat and Linda Parelli.

Pat and Linda love horses, and they love teaching natural horsemanship, which is a way to work with your horses without whipping them or being harsh in any way. Essentially it's a way of teaching communication between you and your horse. The Parellis have been widely praised as some of the most successful "horse whisperers" in the world. They truly understand the language of horses, and they work to improve human-equine relationships by teaching other people that complex language. What they actually teach is how to communicate with the horse using horse language, human body language and the communications horses use among each other.

By doing this, you can develop a relationship with your horses where they begin to trust you. Pat and Linda had been working with horses for years and loved it. They took what they had learned and they imagined something many, many times bigger than anything they had ever done before. They imagined they would teach their methods to the world – not at their ranch in Colorado, but all over the world.

In other words, they used their imaginations to create a vision. Then they took their vision and blew it up in their imaginations.

They took something most people would say couldn't make money: teaching other people about horses. And they said, "We're going to expand our vision into something much bigger – and we'll make money doing what we love to do most."

They imagined a way to do it. They imagined all the details. And now they go around all over the United States,

Canada, Australia and Europe, teaching people in all thesecities and countries about their natural horsemanship techniques.

When I went to my local fair for a two-day program in the outdoor arena to see Pat and Linda, they arrived in a fleet of enormous semi trucks. The trucks were chrome-plated with huge elaborate pictures all over the sides, depicting horses and various scenes of horse training. Every square inch of these trucks was covered with glossy, stunning graphics. When those immaculate and beautiful trucks drive down the road, you can't miss them. You turn to look at them, and you know you are looking at serious wealth.

> # Pat and Linda Parelli have made millions doing what they love most. For information, visit www.parelli.com.

Anyway, these trucks pulled up to the fairgrounds, and the first thing I thought upon seeing this spectacle was, "Wow, this has to be a mega-million dollar operation." Then the horses come out of these trucks, and with them came the people. It wasn't just Pat and Linda; they have several crews of people. They begin unpacking not just the horses and horse stuff, but they also have products to sell – tables and tables of products.

They have books, CDs, and DVDs. They offer training packages with class levels from one to four. And they have all kinds of supplies, even a patented training stick. All told, they have millions and millions of dollars worth of stuff. At first, I didn't want to buy anything. I just wanted to see what they had to teach. By the end of the first day, I was in line buying everything they had available. I bought it all, because I wanted to learn to do everything their way.

I probably wouldn't have been so enthusiastic if I hadn't seen them in action with their horses, using their method. When I saw what they could do with horses, I was amazed. Pat would sit on his horse and he told his horse "Go pee," and his horse would pee. He told his horse to lie down, and the horse did it. The horse followed every command.

He would ride his horse bareback with no bit in its mouth and no reins, and he could get that horse to jump and do all sorts of things with him on its back. And I don't know if you've ever seen people try to load a horse in a trailer when the horse didn't want to go in, but it can take an hour or more. I've seen people whipping horses, having five or six people roping the horse and pushing and pulling the poor beast, all in an effort to get it into a trailer.

Do you know what Pat and Linda do? They'll park a trailer 100 feet away, and they'll tell their horse to go get in the trailer. The horse runs and jumps into the trailer all by itself – no ropes, no nothing.

I saw that what the Parellis have done with horses is incredible. And it was providing great value for me, because I owned a horse and I wanted to learn with my horse the techniques that these people had shown me they had done with their horses.

That's why I ran up to be first in line to buy every one of their products. And I'll tell you, their method works. I began training my horse, and within a week, I saw amazing results.

The point, of course, is that Pat and Linda Parelli took something that would make most people say, "You can't make money doing that!" And they have created a multi-million dollar business. It's not just local to their state or even to the country they live in. They have formed an international business doing what they love to do more than anything in the world. They bring value to millions of people and make millions of dollars doing it.

You can do the same thing. So if you ask me, "Where do I start? How do I go about making millions of dollars? Do I buy real estate? Do I get into the stock market? Do I do Internet marketing?"...well, I say, "The answer is inside you."

You are the one to whom you should be asking these all-important important questions:

1. What is it that you love doing most?
2. What is it you would do, even if you weren't getting paid?

> # Only you can decide what it is you love doing most, and would be doing even if you weren't getting paid to do it.

I listened to Pat and Linda Parelli talk about their horse experiences, and how they got into this business. Pat said that after they had been in business a while and had made millions of dollars, they came to a point where they had a decision to make. Now that they were independently wealthy – and they still loved horses as much as ever – what was it they wanted to do with the rest of their lives?

Pat says he talked to Linda. They sat on the couch one evening and said, "Well, we could buy the biggest ranch you could ever imagine and have servants all over the ranch to take care of everything. We could have horses, barns and stables. We could travel and do whatever we want – we could even sell or close down the business and just sit back and relax the rest of our lives. We could have fun and spend our money as fast as we wanted and we would never run out.

"But is that what we really want to do – or do we want to keep running the business?"

It was a very short conversation, because they both realized they were doing what they loved to do more than anything, and they didn't want to quit doing it. So they decided just to continue doing the business and blow it up 1,000 times bigger – and that is just what they did.

That's what you can do with whatever it is you love to do – whether it's karaoke, writing books, inventing or selling a product, teaching classes or courses, working with children or seniors or the disabled, working with computers and technology…the list is endless. It could be painting, singing, speaking; indeed, it could be anything. Whatever it is you love to do, *imagination* is the way to figure out how to take what you love and bring value to millions of people in the world so you can become a millionaire.

I know a lot of women (and some guys) who just love to shop. What if you're one of them? Let's say you come to me and say, "Paul, the only thing I love to do is shop. I *love* shopping but obviously, I'm not going to *make* money doing that – I'm just going to be expending money. So I guess I have to figure out a way to make millions of dollars so I can keep shopping without worrying about the price tag. I want to be able to buy anything I want. I want to go to Saks Fifth Avenue and Nordstrom and Neiman Marcus and Tiffany and all those fancy stores. I want to be able to buy anything I want, anywhere. I want to buy $3,500 shoes and $6,000 bracelets. I don't even care about having the stuff… I just love shopping!"

Well, have I got a story for you. First of all, I would never try to talk you out of your passion. Instead I would say, "Use your imagination! If shopping is what you truly love to do, how can you use that to create millions of dollars?"

> # There are people who love shopping so much that they've gotten rich doing it. So don't assume that there's no way you can make money doing what *you* love.

A woman I met has done just that. A few months ago, I went back to New York and was there for five days. For three of those days I was meeting with over 100 national TV producers of shows such as *Oprah*, *Live With Regis and Kelly*, *Good Morning America*, various Fox News Network shows, and more. I was there to meet with them face-to-face and talk about how I could put shows together for them.

I had arrived in the Big Apple a couple of days early, but prior to my arrival I had been told about a woman who loves to shop. She has lived and worked in New York for many years, and has been in the modeling business and in media. These days she makes a fantastic living as a personal shopper and image consultant, helping people build wardrobes that will further their success in their businesses, in their careers, and in media appearances. She works with a lot of TV personalities and other celebrities. This woman has developed a terrific reputation for helping people shop and find exactly the right clothes to complement their complexions, the color of their hair and their body types. Whether they're thin or not so thin, she can guide them into choosing the clothes that will make them look their very best on TV.

I'd heard wonderful things about this woman, so I called her and told her I would be visiting New York and I'd like to meet with her. I wanted her to take me shopping. I was glad to pay her $5,000 to take me shopping for five hours in New York. That's a thousand dollars an hour, but I think I got more than my money's worth.

Before she had even met with me, she had already gone to numerous stores picking out items for me to look at. I had spoken with her on the phone at length, and I had sent her photographs. She knew what I looked like, she knew my shoe size, suit sizes, my pant and shirt sizes. She knew what my goals were in speaking on the radio and being on TV. She knew the type of speaking I do – casual speaking as well as formal; sometimes I speak to small groups and sometimes to larger groups and churches. She knew there were many different groups of people who were going to see me, so she figured out all the different types of clothing I should wear for each occasion.

In other words, she had a pretty good idea of who I was. And by the time I got to New York and met with her, she had already picked out a lot of the items. On the day I talked with her I was in Seattle at a trade show. I hopped on a plane straight from the trade show to New York, where I met her in the morning – and we shopped all day.

I was exhausted, but it was fabulous and wonderful, because, as I said, she had everything picked out. I went into the changing rooms to try the items on, and I liked – and bought – virtually everything she had picked out. Now, understand that the $5,000 I had paid her wasn't for the clothes – you have to pay extra for the clothes. The $5,000 was merely her fee for picking out all the clothes and taking me shopping, and giving me her advice about how they looked on me.

Hard work? For some people, maybe – but this lady loves shopping. She loves picking out the clothes and she loves spending money. And do you know what she loves even better than spending her own money? Yep, you guessed it: spending *other* people's money. She has figured out a way to take something she loves to do more than anything on God's green earth, and to get paid for it. In fact, she gets paid *a lot* of money for it. I met her in the morning and we shopped from 10:00 until about 3:00, with me spending thousands of dollars for all those clothes.

I paid her the fee of $5,000 and then we went to eat, and then I went back to my hotel. She went on to meet her second customer that day and shopped for another five hours for another $5,000 – so she got to go shopping all day and pick out all kinds of great clothes and spend other people's money to buy *their* clothes. She was paid $10,000 that day to shop.

> # Can you imagine getting paid several thousand dollars for a few hours of doing what you love to do more than anything on earth?

If you're a person who absolutely loves shopping, can you imagine being paid $10,000 a day to be able to shop and buy all this stuff, and find all these great things for other people? Along the way, she found stuff she liked too, of course. While she was with me she bought herself a pair of cool jeans that she had been hoping to find.

The point is, you can take something as far-fetched as shopping and can imagine ways to make incredible amounts of money doing it. You still don't think you can do it? Well, would you have ever believed that people would pay $5,000 a day to have you be their personal shopper? Did you even know something like that existed?

That's the point of this entire book: to open up your mind and teach you that there are all kinds of opportunities to make money, if you *imagine the possibilities* of what you can do to create money for yourself.

Do you remember the story in a previous chapter about the small, poor village where Average Joe and Rich Dude accepted the challenge to bring water to their village? Average Joe made a little money working hard every day. Rich Dude made an incredible amount of money using his imagination to create a great idea.

And that's how all wealth starts.

Think it and feel it!

You too can create wealth by thinking about what it is that you love to do – by truly imagining the possibilities. And you can make your imagination even stronger, and yourself even more motivated, by making an extra effort to infuse the images you create with positive emotions. So don't just *think* about the fun ways you're going to create your wealth and freedom – really *feel* the pleasure that your new life will bring you. *Feel* the deep sense of satisfaction that you get from knowing you are bringing something of immense value to hundreds, thousands, perhaps millions of people. *Feel* the exhilaration of realizing that something you find to be immense fun is making you incredibly wealthy. *Feel* the giddy delight that comes whenever you tell yourself, "Wow, I can't believe people are paying me to have so much fun!"

Feel the profound relief of waking up early on a cold and rainy morning and knowing you can snuggle back under the covers if you wish, because there's no alarm clock compelling you to get up and brave the weather and the stalled traffic to get to some hopelessly dull or profoundly stressful office job. In fact, if you want to, you can move to some tropical sweet spot where it's *never* cold and rainy! *Feel* the sublimely sensuous pleasure of a tropical sun and cool sea breeze on your bare skin, as you listen to the sound of ocean waves and, perhaps, a distant steel-drum band playing a catchy calypso tune. And *feel* the secret sense of triumph inspired by the knowledge that you are making more money in a few hours on this splendid beach than you ever made in a week or more in your old life as an office drone.

> # Don't just *imagine* your wonderful new life – really *feel* the pleasure that such a life will bring.

So Step 4 in its entirety is: Imagine – *and feel* – the possibilities.

As important as feeling is, it is impossible for me to overstate the importance of imagination in this equation. All the things that are created in the world and in the universe came from imagination – whether they are manmade or natural. If you believe in God or some sort of Supreme Being, you no doubt believe this Being created all things – and before that creation, it had to be imagined.

Even if you don't believe in God, you know that all manmade things had to be imagined first. And so, in a very real sense, *IMAGINATION IS THE SEED OF ALL REALITY.*

Therefore, if you want to change your reality, you first have to plant the seed of imagination – and not just for what you want, but for how you're going to get there. Consider the example of Rich Dude, who became a very rich man by bringing water to his community. If all he had done was think of the idea, but had taken no action to turn that idea into reality, it would have been nothing more than a great idea.

He had to think, "What are the steps I will take? I have to get a loan for materials and labor, I have to line up the construction crew, I have to get permits. Then I have to begin constructing this project, and then it has to go through all of that testing…" So he had to imagine the hundreds and thousands of details that needed to be worked out in order to make his dream a reality. But it all started by imagining the vision he wanted, and imagining all the details that would have to be addressed in order to make that vision a reality. And almost certainly, Rich Dude put some emotion into his imaginings. He imagined the sense of satisfaction that would come from knowing he had solved a very urgent problem for his village. Perhaps he imagined the sense of triumph from knowing that his idea was far more clever than Average Joe's, and that he would be the one to "win" the challenge. And who could blame him if he also felt a big thrill when envisioning all of those far-flung places he would finally get to see once he had scads of money and free time?

Imagination is the seed of all reality. All man-made things first existed in someone's imagination.

So what is it that you want to imagine for *your* life? If you want to become wealthy, if you want to be a millionaire next year or a billionaire in five years, what is it you're going to imagine you do to turn yourself into that millionaire or that billionaire?

I want you to continue to ask yourself this question, but I'm guessing that you are probably already well on your way to finding the answer. And that's terrific. But even if you haven't quite formulated your answer, don't give up. Keep asking yourself these important questions and you will find the answer.

Meanwhile, we'll move to Step 5 in my Formula For Becoming A Millionaire. In the next chapter, I will show you how to use that wonderful imagination of yours to begin believing in yourself in such a way that you are guaranteed to reach any goal you set for yourself.

And you don't have to be an Einstein to do it.

**Imagination is the power
that can turn the world upside down.
It can turn lives around.
It can transform a person who has
next to nothing
into a millionaire
or billionaire.
How will you use this
incredible power you have?
What will you imagine
for *your* life?**

**"Imagination
is more powerful
than knowledge."**
~ *Albert Einstein*

*People don't fail because
they don't have enough belief,
but because they have
the wrong kind of belief.*

*Learn to believe in a brave new way ~
and at a level so powerful,
and so compelling,
that what you believe
becomes reality.*

STEP 5

BELIEVE
At A Bold New Level

This chapter explains the fifth principle in my seven-part Formula For Becoming A Millionaire: BELIEVE AT A BOLD NEW LEVEL. Among other things you will learn:

1. *The difference between merely believing – and creating a belief so powerful that it becomes your reality*
2. *How believing translates to action – and how you can cultivate the kind of belief that translates into action that will make you wealthy*

As you start to change your thinking about wealth (and the wealthy); as you begin to define and focus your desires; as you learn to use your imagination and your emotions to build a grand vision for your life… you will probably start getting pretty pumped, maybe even a little impatient. You might wonder when I'm going to get down to the nitty-gritty and begin sharing some practical advice about some things you can actually *do* to get wealthy. Be patient; that's coming. It's important to remember that you have to truly change your "inner" reality in order to effect any meaningful changes in your "outer" reality. And before we get to the "external" stuff, we need to cover one more important "internal" tool. This is the one tool that can make you or break you.

That tool is *believing*.

The standard American dream... booooring!

Most people get what they believe they will get in their life. Most believe that once they are finished with their schooling and have graduated into the "real" world...

1. They will get a job where they go to work every day, earning a good day's wage for a good day's work.
2. They will continue to work until retirement age, at which time they will retire and begin collecting Social Security, and perhaps whatever pension or retirement plan their company offers, if they are so fortunate.

And that's exactly what most people do. They work hard their entire life, because they believe they *have* to work hard to earn a good living.

It's all part of the American dream, and to most people, the biggest material part of that dream is home ownership. Most people in this country hope and expect that they will someday own their home; it will be their biggest asset. And that too becomes the reality for many.

Why does it become their reality? The answer is simple: because it is exactly what they believed would happen. That belief came first, followed by a lifetime of actions, day after day after day, that were geared towards one thing: making the belief a reality.

Of course, not everyone raised to believe in this common version of the American dream actually manages to make that belief a reality. Some people, for various reasons, can't seem to hold down a job for any length of time. Some people have steady jobs but do not or cannot become homeowners. Some are simply so mired in profound poverty, illness, addiction or some other adversarial situation that they can't or don't rise above their circumstances. Nevertheless, even most of those who don't live the traditional "middle-class" American dream still believe in it at some level. They (or their relatives or friends or society in general) may even believe that they are failures for not living up to the ideal. The "common" version of the American dream is woven so deeply into our fabric that even people who are not actually living the dream generally accept its status as the ideal without question.

I happen to think that anyone who embraces that "common version" is setting his or her sights way too low.

Millionaires have a DIFFERENT American dream

Millionaires and billionaires – and virtually all people who are truly prosperous in life – believe something entirely different from the standard-issue American dream. What they believe is almost the direct opposite of the maximum-work/minimal-reward scenario.

The truly wealthy DO believe...

1. That they don't need to have a job in order to make a living – in fact, having "a job" can prevent you from ever achieving true wealth and success.
2. That they can own cars, houses, vacation homes and real estate in all the hot spots in the world.
   (And maybe they will even have their own private jets to fly them to these locations.)
3. That they can make money while they sleep or vacation.
4. That they don't have to work hard to get ahead – way ahead! But they DO believe that if they're going to put

a lot of time and energy into something, it should be something they absolutely love doing.

The wealthy *don't* believe in such a thing as retirement in the conventional sense, where they work for a few decades and then one day stop working, and live on a fixed income for the rest of their days, playing Bingo or shuffleboard or just whiling away their remaining time on Earth. But they *do* believe in cultivating as much free time as they desire to do all of the things they love – no matter how old or how young they are.

Do you see what a huge difference there is between the "millionaire's American dream" and everyone else's?

(As you believe, so shall you receive)

The millionaire version becomes reality for a few *because they first believed it*. That's what this chapter is about: believing. This is the fifth principle in my seven-step Formula For Becoming A Millionaire. How do you create a belief so powerful that it becomes your reality? That's what we're going to talk about right here, right now – before we get to the "external" stuff. It is a very important principle in The Formula, because *what you believe you're going to get is what you're going to get*.

The problem most people face is that, as I noted above, they have set their sights far too low, as a result of the beliefs about work and wealth that they were raised with. As you know if you've read this far in the book, I have proposed a different way of thinking about money, about rich people, about work. Even though on the surface you might have begun to change your own thinking about these matters, however, those old beliefs (and the resulting habits) can be very hard to break. I want to help you break them so you can learn to harness the remarkable power of belief, and turn it to your advantage.

You have to believe
YOU CAN MAKE IT HAPPEN.

Anything is possible when you believe you can make it happen.
I worded that differently from the way that most people do.
Most people say anything is possible if you have enough belief,
but I say, "Anything is possible when you believe you can make
it happen."

That's right: *You can make it happen.*

The difference between "having enough belief" and
believing *you can make it happen* is the difference between:

+ The person who wishes for a raise – and the one who
  says, "I'm going to give myself that raise!"
  (and does so)

+ The person who hopes to one day be in management –
  and the person who builds and owns a multi-million
  dollar company

+ The person who hopes for enough money to pay the
  bills this month – and the one who creates wealth
  every minute of every day, even as while sleeping or
  sitting on the beach in Hawaii

This crucial difference in belief is the difference between
merely believing in a divine influence that exists in the universe… and believing that *you* are an integral part of that divine
influence.

And that is all the difference in the world… or make that,
in the universe!

Rev up your "belief engine"... and drive right out of that ho-hum existence!

If you have a job, then you probably also have a very high level of belief that you will go to work today. You will go to work because you believe that is the only way you will be able to earn your wage, whatever that is.

Those specific beliefs spur you to a specific sequence of actions. You'll set your alarm clock when you go to bed, you'll get up in the morning, you'll get dressed, you'll eat breakfast, you'll drive or take the subway to work, and you will take the stairs or the elevator to your office, because you believe that by so doing, you will earn money that day.

Guess what? You *will* earn money that day. You'll earn your wage, because you had a belief that you would. You had a special kind of belief – the kind that spurs you to action, causing that thing upon which you focus your desire to become your reality.

You had a belief that you would earn money that day – and your belief was so powerful that you took a number of steps to get yourself up, go to work and to go through the day doing the job that you intended to do, in order to earn the money that you desired.

Your belief was, as I said, a special kind of belief – the kind that prompted you to action and mandated that you would get what you expected to receive. That's an example of true belief. It's the kind of belief that keeps you going to the office day after day, week after week, year after year, until retirement.

"Well, gee, Paul, that sounds kind of depressing," you say. I agree!

But here's the good news. This special type of belief, pow-
ered by imagination and enhanced by emotion, is also the type
of belief that...

+ makes millionaires
+ makes Olympic athletes become gold medal winners
+ makes the real estate entrepreneur become a billionaire

And that is precisely the type of belief I am talking about
in this chapter. If you go to work every day, you already have
the "infrastructure" in place. You're already utilizing this special type of belief. The problem is that you're using it to create
a ho-hum life for yourself (while perhaps making someone else
incredibly wealthy), when *you can do so much better than that*. I
want you to know that you have the ability within you to boost
your existing power of belief in such a way that will propel you
from a mundane life of work and worry to one of extraordinary
wealth and freedom. You simply need to rev up your "belief
engine," and I'm going to show you how to do that.

How belief works
(and DOESN'T work)

Not many people seem to understand the way belief really
works. Most folks seem to think that believing something will
happen simply means you wish or hope or pray it's going to
happen, or you meditate or visualize about it happening. If
you wish and hope and pray and meditate and visualize long
enough or intently enough, the thinking goes, it *will* happen.

I think this is the major area where many people misin-
terpreted the message of *The Secret*. It's easy to see where the
confusion came from – apart from the fact that *The Secret*,
which was taken from many, many hours of interviews with
nearly thirty people, had to be edited and pared down to fit a
feature-length movie format. It is possible that some of the more
complex concepts about the Law Of Attraction were somewhat

diminished as a result. But it's also possible that wishful thinking on the part of many who watched *The Secret* was also to blame for some of the confusion. To tell the truth, I think that at times most of us have wished we could have something for nothing, and if we're honest we'll admit to that. Apparently some people decided that *The Secret* conveyed the too-good-to-be-true message that getting something for nothing on a consistent basis is indeed possible. These people concluded that if they just focused their minds intently enough on whatever they wanted – whether it was a new car, a big house, or the lover of their dreams – the magic Universe Genie would grant their wishes.

Well, as Dr. Phil McGraw would say, "And how's that working out for you?" I imagine that most people, if they are honest (and not profiting from perpetuating the illusion), would answer, "Um... not too well!"

Imagine what would happen if, when the alarm clock went off in the morning, you turned it off and said, "You know, today I'm just going to stay home. I'm going to meditate and visualize getting my paycheck today for today's work. I've used up all my sick time, vacation time and personal time for the year...and, yeah, I have bills to pay, but I know that if I *believe* hard enough, and if I meditate enough and visualize right, that money will come to me. Better yet, I'm going to make myself a vision board of me receiving the money in the mail *today* so that I can pay my bills. But I'm not going to go to work. I'm just going to believe hard enough."

I have the feeling that no matter how long you meditate, how earnestly you visualize, and how elaborate your vision board is, that check you are hoping for isn't going to arrive that day, or the next, or the next. If you hang on to this mentality and continue to stay home meditating and making vision boards, you will probably lose your job and may even end up going broke – but you're definitely not going to become a millionaire.

Now, I'm not suggesting that miracles don't happen. In fact, I've experienced a few of those myself – but in my experience, most of the time you make millions of dollars not by holding on to that magical-thinking, I-don't-have-to-lift-a-finger kind of belief, but by having *a completely different kind.*

The type of belief I'm talking about is what we just talked about: the type that impels you to take action to make the things you desire happen. It's the type of belief with which you are no doubt already familiar. It causes you to set your alarm clock at night, get up and go to work in the morning, work through the day and earn your wage for the day.

So why aren't you rich?

It's because you are not using that belief to its full potential.

(**Why aren't you RICH?**)

What I want to teach you how to do is to take that same type of belief and transform it into a belief that will spur you to earn $1 million, $2 million, $10 million, $100 million… or more. It works exactly the same way as what you're used to, but *it only works when you have the same confidence, and the same level of belief, that impels you to take the required action* – knowing that when you do, you'll receive what you desire.

When you go to work, you know what to do in order to earn your current wage. The belief you need to have to earn a million dollars in a year involves knowing what action you're going to take that will *guarantee* you a million dollars. When you have that level of belief, there's no doubt, no second guessing, no hoping, no wishing and no wondering whether it's going to happen.

When you get up in the morning and go to work, you absolutely know 100% that you will work through the day and earn your wage for the day. The millionaires and billionaires in

the world have the exact same level of confidence and belief in themselves that they will earn millions of dollars this year, because they know that the actions they are taking will *guarantee* that they receive millions of dollars.

Miracles happen, but sometimes they need a little nudge

I'm not saying anything is wrong with connecting with the power of the universe and aligning yourself with whatever it is that you might think of as your higher power or God. Quite the contrary: when you do so, things happen more quickly for you. Miracles begin to happen every day. (In some cases, it may just be that you are more open to noticing miracles when they *do* happen; we've discussed that earlier and will talk about it again in just a little while.)

As I've said before, I'd be the last one to deny that miracles happen, because I've had them happen to me on numerous occasions. At least they seemed like miracles to me, so for all practical purposes, they were. So I'm not denying that when you set a desire for yourself and believe in the power of the universe, things begin to happen in your favor. What I *am* saying is without taking action, you will never achieve the level of wealth that you hope to achieve.

> **Without taking action, you will never achieve the level of wealth that you hope to achieve**

True belief creates action, and belief without action is not real belief. The belief that I'm talking about here has helped me phenomenally through my life. It's the belief that I began implementing in my school days and in my early career. It's the belief that gave me raises and promotions. How? *It spurred me to the actions that caused those promotions and raises.*

When you have the type of belief I'm talking about, you will take the actions that make the visions you have for your life a reality. This is the kind of belief that will make you become an owner of a company, if that's what you desire. It's the belief that will put you on television, if that's your dream. It's the belief that will help you become successful in singing or painting or selling real estate, or whatever it is you love to do.

(Belief + Action = Miracles)

If you love horses, it's the belief that can make you a phenomenal success in the horse industry, making millions of dollars. Whatever your passion is, when you use this level of belief that spurs you on to take action, it will make you millions and millions of dollars. And when you look at your life and all you have achieved – particularly in comparison to where you were just a few short years ago – it will indeed seem like a miracle.

I want to tell you a story that, in all honesty, might be an urban legend. At least the details have yet to be verified by any news outlet that I'm aware of (blogs and online discussion forums don't count). I'm telling this story because it illustrates an important point. This is a tale of a man who worked as a repairman for a refrigeration company, maintaining the refrigerated railroad cars that carry frozen foods. Late one afternoon, shortly before quitting time for the railroad workers, he went into a boxcar to check the system and make sure that everything was working properly for the next day. For some reason, the door closed behind him and he found himself trapped inside the car.

According to the story, it was about 4:00 PM when he got locked in. When 4:30 rolled around, all the workers in the train yard went home – all, that is, except for this poor guy, who was trapped inside of the car, believing that the refrigeration unit was working enough to make it unbearably cold inside.

He began to get cold, fully believing that he was going to freeze to death before anyone could free him the next morning. Judging form the marks found in the car, he began pounding on the metal walls with his tools, no doubt hoping that there was somebody outside who would hear him and let him out. But there was nobody around; they had all gone home.

He lay there, getting colder and colder as the hours went by. By late evening, he was beginning to lose hope that anybody would hear him, but he continued to pound on the side of the boxcar, hoping that somebody would hear him, but they didn't. As he got colder and more tired, the possibility – no, probability – of his death became increasingly more real to him.

He dug around in his toolbox until he found some small scraps of paper and a pencil, and he began to write a note to his wife and family in case he didn't make it out alive. He wrote something to the effect of, "I'm trapped in this car and I'm freezing to death. I'm afraid I will die, and this is the last time I'll have a chance to tell you how much I love you."

The stronger your belief, the greater your accomplishments

According to the story, some time after he wrote out the note, he lay down and died. The next morning when the workers came in, they found him dead in the refrigeration car. The coroner took him away and performed an autopsy on him; the autopsy report came back and confirmed that he actually had frozen to death. His organs had shut down, and circulation to his extremities had been virtually cut off as his body tried to protect its core functions and retain as much heat as possible.

Everything in his autopsy report was consistent with death from hypothermia.

(The deeper your fear, the greater your trials)

The interesting point about this story is that the refrigeration unit in the car was not working, and the outside temperature had only gotten down to about 60°. The temperature inside the car was about the same.

The man would not have frozen to death had it not been for one tiny but highly significant detail: he *believed* that he was freezing to death. He believed this so strongly that his body reacted to his belief in exactly the same way as it would have reacted to a life-threatening drop in temperature.

I'll grant you that this is an amazing story. And even if it is nothing more than an urban legend, I have a feeling that it's based on a true event whose exact details have been lost in constant repetition. More importantly, this tale describes a phenomenon that is anything but uncommon. Throughout human history many cultures have embraced the concept of the "curse." Some cultures believe that if a victim of a curse knows about it and accepts that he or she is doomed, the power of the curse increases and the person contributes to his or her own demise. In some cultures in the Caribbean, people have reportedly sickened and died simply because someone put a curse on them, and they believed so strongly in the curse's power. In our own contemporary culture, we generally consider ourselves to be too sophisticated to believe in curses, but it is pretty well accepted that our thoughts and beliefs can have a significant influence on our physical well-being, for better or worse. And, of course, the placebo effect has been well documented in medical research.

So whether or not the story about the man who "froze" to death is literally true, there is no denying the power of belief. The important point – and my whole reason for telling the story above – is that the same type of belief that can cause a person to give up all hope *is precisely the type of belief that can restore hope and inspire a person to create an amazing life.* The same kind of belief that can make someone physically ill is the kind of belief that, if turned around, can create glowing good health. And the same kind of belief that keeps you going to work every day to maintain your stable but essentially unsatisfying life is the kind of belief that, if channeled properly, can spur you to action, make you a lot of money and get you out of the position you're in. If you don't like your job, this type of belief will cause you to do whatever is necessary to create opportunities to begin doing what you're passionate about.

> # What kind of belief will you choose? One that builds, or one that destroys?

In the last chapter I told you about a woman who was passionate about karaoke. She loved singing karaoke, she loved mentoring and training people how to do karaoke and work with the sound systems. People like her who get hold of a dream – and a passion – can become a phenomenal worldwide success.

Yes, it's people like her… and people like you.

It doesn't really matter what your passion is – whether it's karaoke, real estate, teaching, singing, painting or even selling cars. Whatever is your passion in life, when you get hold of it and apply this level of belief to it, you can create success that's unlimited. *This* is what generates those amazing success stories. It's what creates the dotcom successes, the "overnight" sensations and the millionaires and billionaires who exist in the world today.

Belief and passion are what drive the people who create the movies you watch, the people who put together the real estate deals so big that they are featured on the nightly news, the people who lead the cities that grow when other areas' economies are taking horrific hits, the developers who build the buildings, and all of the movers and shakers in the other industries that you read about. The *Forbes* list of the top 500 wealthiest people in the world is made up of people who have this level of belief, who know with absolute certainty that they're not relying upon some abstract notion that the universe is going to take care of them.

These people may very well believe that God (or the universe) will provide for them, but they also know that the universe and God operate *through* them, and that they have within themselves the intelligence, consciousness, desire and willpower needed to change their lives. They may believe in miracles, but they also know that their beliefs and actions play a big part in creating those miracles.

Belief can make you or break you

When you recognize that you have the power within you to change your life, that changes everything. You begin to recognize that you have within yourself the ability to create millions of dollars, because you have ideas and imagination. As we talked about in the last chapter, you can take those ideas and imagination to come up with a plan for your life. At the core of it all, however, is belief – and more specifically, belief in yourself. Belief is required to become successful, belief is required to create millions of dollars, but it's the level of belief in *yourself* that spurs you on to take action.

It's not just what you believe, but how strong your belief is

There were times in the past when I felt that my life was collapsing all around me. I discussed some of this in my Introduction, as well as in my first book, *Secrets Of The Miracle Inside*, but I bring it up here because it is directly related to some of the points I want to make about belief. It wasn't that I didn't have *enough* belief at the time; it was that I was believing in things that weren't true – or at least they weren't true until my beliefs helped make them true! I believed that life was difficult, and it was. I believed that people were against me, and the more I believed that, the more "proof" I seemed to find that my belief was right on target. I even believed that my health was going to suffer because I didn't have time to exercise or eat right. I was certain that sooner or later, it was all going to catch up with me. Guess what? My health started suffering.

Why did my health start suffering? It's simple: because I believed that it was going to, and sure enough, that's what it did.

My eyesight started deteriorating, and I had to get glasses with stronger prescriptions every year. Why? I am convinced that it was because I *believed* my eyesight was deteriorating. I never considered that since I read so much and worked so much on papers in my office, my eyes might just have needed rest. My back also started hurting, and if you've ever had a backache, you know how excruciating *that* pain can be.

In short, I believed that life was a struggle, and by golly, it was. My physical problems were all the proof I needed.

Of course, my beliefs alone didn't cause my problems. They were working in tandem with the actions I took (or failed to take) as a result of those beliefs. The results of my actions did nothing but reinforce my beliefs, which further reinforced the actions, and so on. Life became increasingly more stressful and less enjoyable, and it wasn't getting any better.

(Believe your life is difficult, and it *will be*!)

On the surface I was a success. I had a wonderful job; I was the CEO and owner of a big company. But I was getting little enjoyment from it. I told myself that my position was a stressful and demanding one that required a lot of my time. Since I already believed that I was a workaholic, it followed that I was going to have to put in long hours. When I believed those things, I *did* have to put in long hours and my job *was* stressful. What I believed to be true became my reality. To make things worse, during that same time, I was dealing with a very difficult relationship with my business partners, which made life at the office even more challenging.

I was dealing with problems in my personal life as well. When our young son was diagnosed with autism, that created a whole new mountain of stress. He is a high-functioning autistic, but autistic nonetheless. So my wife and I struggled as parents, trying to understand how to raise him and how to cope with the situations that parents of autistic children so frequently face. It was extremely difficult. In fact, it was the hardest thing I've ever faced, because we all had to deal with very powerful emotions – mine, my wife's and our son's. It was an enormously challenging time in my life.

I believed that life was hard, and that it wasn't ever going to be easy. And life did not fail to live down to my expectations! I will always remember this as a time when all areas of my life were spiraling down on me and I felt that my life was falling apart around me. I didn't want to be at work; I hated my situation there. I didn't want to be home, because I couldn't cope with the family struggles that we were dealing with.

My health continued to fail as well, and to make it worse, during this time I was losing any faith in spirituality, in my sense of the universe, in God. I wondered what my role really was in this whole crazy drama. It was, as I said in my Introduction, truly the proverbial dark night of the soul.

Then a miracle happened, which I wrote about at more length in *Secrets Of The Miracle Inside*. Basically I changed the way I looked at the things in my life. When you change the way you look at things, the things you look at change – the world can change and your situation certainly can change. I began implementing this Step 5, belief: belief in myself, at a level that spurred me to take action to make my life better. I also began to change my erroneous beliefs. The result of these changes was that my actions changed, and therefore my life changed.

I began to believe that life could not possibly be as hard as I was thinking that it was, because if life really *was* that hard, it just wasn't worth living. I began to consider my options:

1. Either life is not worth living…
2. Or I'm looking at it all wrong.

I decided to undertake a grand experiment and ask myself, "What if I *am* looking at life all wrong?" And I began to ask myself some other important questions:

✦ What if I begin to believe the opposite of all the things I previously believed?

✦ What if I begin to believe that life is easy?

✦ What if I begin to believe you can make millions of dollars without having a job?

✦ What if I begin to believe that I can begin acquiring all the real estate I've always wanted to own?

✦ What if I begin to believe that life is full of opportunity every single day and that money can be created with just my ideas?

✦ What if I begin to believe that my health is fabulous – and that I can run hard, ride hard, swim hard and do all the activities that I want?

✦ What if I begin to believe that I eat healthy?

✦ What if I begin to believe that I get restful sleep at night and I wake up full of energy?

✦ What if I begin to believe that I can be wealthy *and* stress-free – that I can create money, have wealth and prosperity and great health without having a job or the stresses in my life?

Just as an experiment, I made a conscious choice to believe all of these things. It certainly couldn't hurt, I reasoned, and it was far better than sitting around wallowing in my misery. To make the experiment worthwhile, though, I knew that the beliefs I chose to embrace had to be something more than mere items on a list. After all, millions of people hope for most or all of those things I had listed. Many of them ask or expect the universe to provide those things, or they pray to God to bring those things to them. All too many cannot imagine actually amassing a fortune of their own creation, so they simply wish, hope, pray, ask or expect to win the lottery.

They meditate about wealth, they visualize it, some create vision boards for themselves; every day they imagine being wealthy – and years later, they're still in the same position they were in, if not worse.

I knew that if my list was to become a reality for me, *I needed a different kind of belief*. I needed the belief that would make me know that it would happen – not just hope that it would happen, not just wish that it would happen and not just sit around waiting for it to happen. I had to *know* it would happen.

How did I get to the point where I knew it was going to happen? The simplest way to put it is that I convinced myself that it was already so. For example, if I wanted to eat healthy, I simply had to believe that I already did eat healthy, and I had to believe it in such a way that my belief would spur me to appropriate action – so that I really *was* eating healthy.

If wishes were winning lottery tickets...

I need to make an important distinction here. This type of belief is not at all the same thing as taking lousy care of yourself and living in denial about it. This is not a situation in which you eat appallingly unhealthy foods, drink and smoke to excess and refuse to exercise – and still tell yourself that you are eating in a healthy way and really taking care of yourself. This isn't what I was doing and it's not what I recommend that you do. I am talking instead about a belief that allows you to *see yourself actually eating healthy foods and practicing other healthy habits* – and your belief spurs you to action to really do these things.

This is what I did. I believed that I would begin changing my diet, that I would begin changing what I bought to eat, and that I would begin eating differently. I actually saw myself doing this. My belief caused me to take action accordingly. That made it a true belief.

I also believed I would begin getting more sleep, because I would go to bed earlier. I would begin not ingesting caffeine during the day, and not having too much chocolate before I went to bed, as I'd noticed that kept me awake too much. And guess what? These beliefs caused me to take action to make them true. I did begin sleeping much better, and I began feeling a lot better as a result. My belief that I was healthy was becoming more than a belief: it was becoming the truth.

And so did my belief that I could become wealthy. I began taking various actions that would make my beliefs about wealth become reality. I started finding ways to access money that I never knew I could access before. I acquired real estate that I'd never previously thought I could purchase.

In short, I began taking action to make my dreams come true.

(**... everyone would be a millionaire!**)

Most notably, my belief that life was *not* hard and *not* stressful starting becoming true. I was becoming healthier and wealthier all the time. Why? I was using this special type of belief, this fifth principle in my Formula For Becoming A Millionaire – not the other type that involves wishing and hoping, but the type where *I was taking action to guarantee the results that I wanted.* I was believing at a bold new level.

What started happening in my life was truly amazing. The stresses all but went away, my health improved, my child's autistic conditions improved dramatically, I even got rid of my glasses. That's right: I no longer need glasses to see.

The pain in my back even got better. Why? I believed I had a strong healthy back and that I would have good posture. Before that, I believed I had poor posture – and I did. (Some might argue that I believed I had poor posture because I actually had poor posture, rather than that I had poor posture because I believed I did. It doesn't matter – the result was the same: I had poor posture!) I believed that eventually this would lead to back problems, and I had back problems. For ten long years I had pain in my back – not consistently, but over ten years I had

reoccurring back pain. I chalked it up as just one of those things that we all deal with as we get older.

(**Accepting a bad situation is a belief...**)

When my back pain went away, I had to rethink that notion. Or, rather, I rethought that notion and my back pain went away.

This led me to wonder why so many people suffer pain in their back and other sorts of aches and pains as they get older. Certainly diet and lifestyle choices, as well as heredity, play some part – but could at least part of the problem be that we are taught to believe aches and pains are an inevitable part of aging? Some of you will probably argue that I'm getting cause and effect confused, and that we believe pain is part of getting older precisely *because* so many middle-aged and older people seem to have chronic pain of one sort or another. And (the reasoning goes) so many people have those pains because it's just a natural part of the process of aging. Well, as was the case with my poor posture and my belief that I had poor posture, the result is the same either way. If we believe that pain is an unavoidable part of getting older, we're less likely to take action to prevent or reverse the conditions that cause the pain. And when the pain begins, or when it gets worse, this only reinforces our belief and our resulting actions.

I think the same may be true with at least some of the eyesight problems so many people have after "a certain age." How many people say, "Well, you know, I'm 48 years old – it's probably time I finally get some reading glasses. I can't read as well as I used to; those numbers and letters get smaller every year!"

Why does nearly everybody who has reached their forties say that? Doctors tell us that it's because of a condition called *presbyopia*, which starts happening around the age of forty or so. We are told it is an inevitable part of aging, so that's what most of us believe. It's going to happen to you, it's going to happen to me, it's just a condition that we accept, so guess what happens?

$$\left(\text{ ...I choose to believe something better is coming. } \right)$$

One day when you're forty-something, or maybe even before, you're having a stressful day, and you suddenly find you can't read as well as you did yesterday. So you say, "Well, I guess it's time for me to get reading glasses." You buy the glasses at your local drug store. As time goes on, your eyes get worse and worse and you have to get stronger and stronger lenses. You may have to go to an eye doctor and get a special prescription.

Why does that happen? Is declining eyesight, particularly close-up vision, really an inevitable part of aging? Or could at least part of the problem be that you were conditioned to believe that this is what would happen, so your body reacts accordingly?

I won't presume to say what is true for other people; I can only speak from my own experience. I do know that I was able to reverse my own eyesight challenges. I can tell you truthfully that once upon a time I had to wear glasses and now I don't. Maybe I will need them when I get older (*much* older, hopefully!), but I am going to take as good care of my eyes as I can, and I'm going to see how long I can put off "the inevitable."

For now, I don't wear my glasses anymore, because I no longer need them. Moreover, I can see things I could not see before. Why? Because I began to believe that I could – and as a result, I began to experiment with my eyes. I began to practice looking at things without my glasses.

I didn't squint and I didn't strain my eyes. I simply began imagining that the stuff I was looking at was clear. By doing that a little bit five or ten minutes every single day, I noticed that sometimes what I was looking at did indeed become clearer. Finally, I recognized that it never was a problem with my eyes; it was always a problem with my *thinking* that caused the poor vision.

When I thought that I could not see, my brain programmed itself *not* to see things clearly, but as I began to believe that I could see things more clearly, and actually began to experiment, I had more moments of seeing very clearly. I recognized that if that was actually happening, it wasn't my eyes that were the problem, but my thinking.

> # Belief can delay or outright prevent much that we deem "inevitable."

As for my back pains, I changed my beliefs and said, "I have good posture," but just saying those words wasn't enough. I also had to have the level of belief that causes results. Remember, *the type of belief that causes results is the type of belief that spurs you to take action to guarantee that you get the results you want.*

If I believe that I have good posture, what action do I have to take to make that belief a reality? Well, first of all, I have to really start paying attention to my posture. I have to start sitting up straight – putting my shoulders and neck back, and doing that several times throughout the day – forming a habit of *giving myself good posture*. This is precisely what I did, and as I did it, my neck pains eventually went away, my back pains eventually went away, and soon a good posture *and* a life free of back pain became reality for me.

Now I don't have back pains, I don't have neck pains, and I have excellent posture.

When my beliefs changed, my life changed.

I applied this type of belief – this fifth principle in my Formula For Becoming A Millionaire – across my whole life, and *everything began to change.* I began to get healthy, my work and family relationships improved, my son's autism improved and I became more successful.

Belief can work for you or against you. Once upon a time, my own beliefs worked against me and made my life utterly miserable. Now I have created beliefs that work in my favor, and I have been able to use them to create a life that is completely amazing.

You can do the same.

Numbers don't lie!

Some of you might be saying, "Well, Paul that's all very interesting, but it's just a matter of perspective. In reality nothing changed. In reality, you changed the way you saw the world, so it looks different to you."

We discussed this matter a little earlier in this book, but I think it's well worth mentioning again. It's true that much of our individual and collective "reality" depends upon our perception – not all, of course, but more than many people think. If we look for only the bad in life, we seem to get more of what we look for. Conversely, when we're more open to seeing the good things, we're more likely to experience them. That's undeniable. However, not every measure of success or effectiveness is purely subjective. Very often there are external or objective indicators that let you know that what you're doing is making a difference.

(If we look for the bad in life,)
we usually find it!

For example, my bank statement doesn't lie. I do know that when I changed the way I thought about money, my finances improved. I began making mass amounts of money. When I believed that I didn't need a job to make a living, I walked away from my job – and at the time I walked away I didn't have any money saved up.

Most people thought I was crazy for doing what I did. As CEO of a multimillion- dollar company, I was making a fabulous salary. Most people would have never walked away from a job like that. Although I got a good deal in the buyout, I left millions of dollars on the table. Why? I believed that I could make millions of dollars more *without* a job. That belief spurred me into action – and I took action to ensure that I could still make a lot of money.

As I noted in my Introduction, I made more money in the first six months of not having any job at all than I would have in an entire year if I had stayed working as a CEO at my former company. And the wealth is still growing. My bank accounts are growing, my real estate holdings are increasing, and my total prosperity picture is improving dramatically. Oh, yes, and my health continues to get better as well.

Numbers don't lie, my bankers don't lie and my financial statements don't lie – so you really cannot say it's only a matter of perspective. Certainly perspective plays a part; after all, changing your perspective is an important first step to changing your life. I had to change my way of looking at things before I could change anything else. But when you begin believing in yourself, and believing that you can change your life, that change becomes a physical reality. It becomes something that is measurable, observable and very "real."

(**If we look for the good,
we usually find it, too!**)

No way out?

My father-in-law has shared a lot of wonderful stories with me about his days in the Air Force. He had amazing opportunities and got to do fascinating things. He got to train in supersonic aircraft and break the sound barrier; he's proud of the fact that not many people can say they've done that.

During previous presidential administrations, he flew large four-engine jet cargo aircraft. He was chosen to fly support for the President and carry the Secret Service, the President's cars and the many items that the President and his entourage would need on their frequent campaigns. During the Vietnam War he flew airlift missions into Vietnam and surrounding countries to bring in food, supplies and needed support equipment.

The stories he tells of the time he was in training intrigue me the most. He was put in a number of different and very challenging situations. Sometimes he and his fellow trainees were placed in decompression chambers to see how they responded to lack of oxygen and radical changes in air pressure. This was to get them used to being at altitude or flying in an airplane at 30,000 feet and then suddenly having a rapid decompression. It was quite an ordeal.

They also put the trainees through land survival and prisoner of war training, creating situations similar to those experienced by downed air crew members behind enemy lines and those captured as prisoners of war. This was so they could learn what it was like to be in the dark for long periods with no food and no communication with the outside world.

My father-in-law says that before they were put in these confinement cells, instructors told them they could not escape. They were told they would be trapped in solitary confinement for a certain period, so they'd better deal with it. Of course it was a test to prepare them for dealing with a real-life P.O.W. situation. How would they handle it? How would they survive? Would they have the capacity to overcome the physical and mental challenges they might face?

Most of the trainees who were put in these cells took the trainers at their word when they said they could not escape, so guess what? They didn't even try to look for a means to escape. My father-in-law was different. He says he has never taken anything people tell him at face value. If someone says there's no way something can be done, that doesn't mean anything to him. In fact, he takes that as a personal challenge to prove there is a way to accomplish the allegedly impossible task.

(Is your life a cage?)

Before he was taken to his small wooden cell, a hood was placed over his head so he couldn't see where he was being taken. After he was put into that tiny cell and the hood was removed, he began to investigate his surroundings. He noticed a small peep hole that the guards would use to look in at the "prisoners." He found that he could also push the small wooden cover of the peep hole sideways with his finger from the inside, allowing him to see the wooden cells directly across from his.

My father-in-law studied how the cells were constructed, how the opening and locking mechanism worked, and how it sealed back up when the door closed. From his prison cell, he carefully observed everything: the door, the lock, the hinges, the height and length of the mechanism on the outside of the cell – in order to devise a way to escape.

(**Let yourself out!
You have the key!**)

My father-in-law began to imagine a way out of his little cell. Of course, he first had to believe there *was* a way out; otherwise, his exercise in imagination would have been a waste of his time and energy. And if there's one thing that you're taught in a captive situation, it's not to squander time or energy.

All of the other soldiers who had gone through this facility believed there really was no way out and that trying to plan a way out was a waste of time. So they never even tried. But my father-in-law believed there *was* a way, so he began to think about it. He began to imagine, based on the observations he'd made, how he might be able to open that lock, release the trigger and get out through that door that he had come in.

He imagined a way, and he began to take action. He believed that by extending his arm through a small access door for food, he would be able to reach the handle for the mechanism that opened the door. He waited until night and he could hear the guard snoring away. Now was his chance. He quietly opened the small access door and slowly slid his arm out of the opening and up toward the handle. Fortunately his arm was long enough to reach, and he had hold of the handle and was just ready to open the cell… when the telephone rang at the guard station.

He immediately pulled his arm back inside, just as he heard the guard saying, "Is that right? Which cell was it?" That's when he realized that there was a closed-circuit television on the cell doors, and that the area was being watched from another location.

Luckily for him, whoever was monitoring the closed-circuit TV couldn't count very well, and gave the wrong location when the guard asked, "Which cell was it?" Three guards immediately descended upon the cell next to my father-in-law's, opened the door, and tortured the neighboring "prisoner" for many hours while my father-in-law lay on the floor of his cell listening. All the while he was thinking to himself, "At least I tried, and I almost made it!" It was a triumph of sorts for him; his unfortunate neighbor, on the other hand, didn't have quite the same view of the situation.

At the debriefing of the POW camp the head instructor asked, "Who was it that tried to escape from the box?" My father-in-law cautiously raised his hand, hoping that his next door prisoner was not close by in that auditorium. The instructor said, "You know, you're the only one who tried to escape from the box. Everyone else believed that it was impossible!"

The point is that when you believe something, it will become your reality. When you believe, as most people do, that you have to work at a job all your life and that you're going to earn a salary, that's what will happen. If you believe life will be difficult, that's what it will be. If you believe that people around you cause stressful situations and you just have to learn to deal with them, then that's what your reality will be. When you believe that you have to work until age 65 or 68 or even 70 before you can possibly retire, than that's what will happen for you, barring a layoff or illness or an early demise.

On the other hand, when you dare to believe that life can be amazing, that life can be fulfilling, that you can be healthy, that you can make millions of dollars while you sleep and while you vacation in Hawaii – then that's the way your life will be.

When you believe that you can own your own private jet if you wish, that you can have all the cars and vacation houses you desire, that you will own real estate in San Francisco, Seattle, Hawaii, New York, or wherever you want... when you believe that to the level that causes you to take action, *then it will become a reality.*

That's the level of belief that all successful people have. That's what makes Olympic athletes into gold medalists, that's what makes an ordinary person a millionaire or a billionaire, and that's what will make you become whatever it is that you want to be.

Don't believe the doubters who insist there is no way out of the small and confining prison cell of an ordinary existence. Instead, dare to look around you: study the metaphorical walls, the ceiling, the doors, the latches, the locks. Use your imagination. Reinforce your imagination with emotion. Adopt and embrace a fierce belief in yourself, *belief on a level that will propel you to take action* to escape. It may very well be easier than you think, for unlike the dismal cells in a real POW camp, that prison you are in is illusory… and just beyond it are the stars.

*The idea inside you
may seem small at first
but as you grow the idea
in your imagination,
what blossoms may amaze you.*

*It is your gift.
Take that gift and grow it even more
and share it with the world
in a big way.*

*And the world in return
will give you wealth
and freedom
and happiness.*

STEP 6

EXCHANGE VALUE On A Large Scale

This chapter explains the sixth step in my seven-part Formula For Becoming A Millionaire: EXCHANGE VALUE ON A LARGE SCALE. Among other things you will learn:

1. *How the principle of value exchange can make you rich (or not!)*
2. *The two kinds of giving, and how both can contribute to making you incredibly wealthy*

We've spent the first five chapters of this book discussing the internal changes you have to make in order to create wealth – the ways you must change your thinking and your perception.

The final two principles in this seven-part Formula will concentrate on the important "external" stuff.

If I were to ask you why you want to become wealthy, what would you tell me? If you're like most people, you might answer with one or more of the items on the following list. And you'll probably come up with one or two things I haven't included.

"Wish list" of the would-be rich:

1. "I want to stop worrying about whether or not I'm going to be able to pay the bills and still have money left over at the end of the month for groceries – to say nothing of any left for the fun stuff!"

2. "I want to stop having to penny-pinch and worry about how much everything costs. I don't just want the large order of fries… I want a prime rib and lobster dinner!"

3. "I want more freedom to do what I want, when I want, without busting my butt going to work every day at a job I hate, and where I never get ahead."

4. "I want a new car… a Ferrari or a Porsche."

5. "I want a vacation home in Hawaii or Florida or the Bahamas. Heck, maybe I even want to be able to buy my own island!"

6. "And while I'm dreaming, I want my own private jet, so I can go anywhere I want, any time I want, without dealing with the hassles of airports."

A tall order? An all-but-impossible dream? Sure it is, if you're stuck in that poverty mentality I've been working for the past five chapters to help you shed! But if I've done my job right so far, you're at least beginning to see that none of the things on the list above are impossible. I'm here not only to tell you that they're all possible, but to show you how you can acquire them. Whatever reasons you may have for wanting to be wealthy, I'm here to teach you how to get there.

Remember the farmer we discussed in an earlier chapter? Like that farmer, you create the life of your dreams by planting the right kinds of "seeds" to get the right kind of "crop." If the crop you want is wealth, money and fancy homes in exotic places like Hawaii, Florida and the Bahamas (or on your own private island), if your dream is to have fancy cars and your own private jets... yes, those are big dreams, but guess what? They are all possible if you plant the right seeds.

If you want a small crop, you plant a small amount of seed. What do you do if you want a bigger crop? It's simple: You plant more seeds. If the seeds that are coming up are not turning into the types of crops you want, what do you do? You plant a different kind of seed.

It's not all that difficult, and to tell the truth, it's most likely quite a bit easier than the processes a farmer has to go through to *literally* increase his crops or plant new crops. Farming is hard work under the best of circumstances, and there's the inescapable fact that the farmer is dealing with more forces beyond his or anyone else's control than the typical millionaire-in-the-making will ever face. Sometimes, no matter what the farmer does – no matter how many seeds he plants and how carefully he cultivates them – nature throws him a curve in the form of drought, storms, fires, disease or insects. Lacking these unfortunate occurrences, however, our farmer gets exactly the quality and quantity of crop he planned for – because he planted the right seeds and tended them in the right way to get the desired result.

$$\left(\textbf{To get a bigger reward, offer greater value.} \right)$$

What we're really talking about here – the gist of principle number six – is how to *exchange the right kind of value to get the right kind of reward.*

If you're not getting the amount of reward you want, you exchange more value to get more reward. It's quite simple, but it's amazing how few people truly understand the principle of value exchange.

It occurs to me that you might be a little puzzled right now, thinking that I am contradicting my previous assertions that

you don't have to work hard to become incredibly wealthy. It may seem that I'm now implying you *do* have to work hard if you want to reap big rewards.

In reality there's no contradiction here. You *don't* have to work hard, but *you do have to have something of value to offer the world*. And if you want to become very wealthy – if you want to demand and receive a lot of value – you have to offer a lot of value. The more value you have to offer, the more value you will get back. But you *don't* have to bust your buns to do this, as you'll see in this and the following chapter.

What are you cultivating?

Many people wish they were rich, and many dream of making millions of dollars effortlessly. In most people's minds, the most effortless way to wealth is to win the lottery. The odds against that happening, though, are pretty steep. It really doesn't matter how much you wish, hope, pray, call on God or Source or the universe, it doesn't matter how many vision boards you make, it doesn't matter if you use your "lucky" numbers or the numbers in the fortune cookie from last night's Chinese dinner. To depend upon the lottery as a guaranteed road to wealth is a fool's game.

I'm certainly not knocking wishes and hopes and dreams and desires, for they are what motivate all of us to want better lives for ourselves and those we love. If you didn't have wishes or dreams or desires, you wouldn't be reading this book, would you? As I've said before, however, wishing and hoping aren't enough. It takes a solid Formula – like this one! – to turn your wishing into reality.

As we've gone through the steps in my Formula, we've talked about changing your thinking about money and wealth. We've discussed focusing your desires so you will get a better idea of exactly what it is you want in your life. Then we went on to talk about imagination, and how you can use imagination to create huge, wonderful, "impossible" ideas about what you're going to do in order to get what you want. As we discussed, you don't have to be exact, for you're playing with your imagination. You're using it to have fun and *imagine all the possibilities*. Without imagination, however, you can never get to the place you want.

Once you have imagined what is possible, that possibility is like a seed that begins taking root. You begin cultivating and growing it. You nurture it with positive emotions, which act as both sunlight and water to make it grow. And as you continue to nurture it, it grows, blossoms and thrives in the fertile field that is your mind. While you are growing your ideas, you are also nurturing something else: a belief in yourself and a belief that everything you want to happen will happen – a belief so strong that it spurs you to take the actions to create your new life of wealth, health and happiness.

Belief leads to action, which further encourages belief.

Are you starting to see how all of the principles in this Formula can work, individually and together, to make you a millionaire?

Let's backtrack a little and talk about ideas. I've met many people who have ideas, but they don't cultivate them, or they don't cultivate them to their fullest potential. They have planted the seeds and perhaps they are nurturing them, but they planted a small crop. And they are dissatisfied or disappointed with the yield.

Not long ago I met a woman who was the teacher of her own private school. She had taken an idea and cultivated it into a reality. She was currently teaching about thirty children at this school, and she was working with the families of these children as well. Yet she wasn't satisfied; she wanted something more.

She said to me, "I've got this great school going. I've cultivated this idea. I've done a lot of the things you're telling me how to do, but I'm not making a lot of money and I don't understand why."

I said, "I'll tell you why. You know the idea that we talked about regarding exchanging value? Well, you have to do it on the level of what you expect to receive from it. If you want millions of dollars out of it then you need to put millions of dollars worth of value into it."

"What do you mean?" she asked. "How could I possibly do that?"

I replied, "I mean that if you want millions of dollars, you can't teach just thirty children and expect that thirty families will fund your retirement. If you want to get rich by teaching, then you have to provide value worth millions of dollars. You either need a few people who are willing to pay you millions of dollars in return for what you're providing – or you need to provide your products and services to a lot more people."

> # If you want millions of dollars, create millions of dollars worth of value.

I knew I had her interest now, so I continued, "Look, you obviously have the knowledge, wisdom and experience to teach children. Well, think about the ways you could expand that to many more people. Remember, if the farmer wants more crops he plants more seed. So if you want more return for your teaching experience and knowledge, then you need to expand it to influence more children and more families. You need to teach more children – but there are limits to how many you can teach in one location. Maybe you could expand the model of your educational system and duplicate schools all over the country. In addition to or even instead of the schools, you could have an online store where you offer products based on your methods. You can have teleseminars and the like. The more people you reach – and the more value you offer – the more you will get in exchange."

I explained to her that by providing more value to more people, she was giving to the world, so she could ask for a bigger return. When you provide more value, you can ask for – and receive – more value in exchange.

And that's the whole point about exchanging value: Once you've focused your desire and imagined the possibilities, *you have to find a way to provide the maximum amount of value to the maximum number of people, in order to receive the maximum award.*

Quid pro quo

How are *you* going to exchange value? What is the value you're going to give in exchange for what you want? Nothing is free; the world is in equilibrium. You don't get something for nothing. If you want something, you have to give something. That's the literal meaning of the Latin term, *quid pro quo*: "something for something."

When you get up and go to work you want your paycheck, but you're not going to get your paycheck unless you get up and go to work every day of the week. The value you're giving is a day's work, and you get a day's wage. If you're happy with your day's wage, that's great; keep on doing what you're doing. But then, if you were happy with your day's wage you probably wouldn't be reading this book. If you're not happy with the wage you're getting, how can you change it? The answer is that you change it by *giving more value*. Right now, you're giving value to your company one day at a time. You're providing a service – your time – and you're exchanging your time for a paycheck.

How can you create more value? You do it by giving more value to more people. Right now, you're doing it for one company, and it's worth a certain amount of money in the market-place. If you want more money, you're probably not going to get much more money from your company, because you're still giving the same amount of value.

Sure, you can increase it a little bit; for example, you could become a supervisor or a manager in your company. That's worth more money because you're creating more value. Suppose you become a supervisor of five people. You're creating more value because now you're helping five other people do their jobs. You're helping to coordinate and organize those five people. Therefore, your value for your company just increased. You can ask for more money when you take on the new responsibilities of becoming a supervisor for five people. (Now, I know some of you will point out that there are some companies that don't properly reward their employees when they take on more responsibility. I'm just talking about the way things should be. And if your company *doesn't* reward you according to the value you provide, I'd say that's even more reason to find a way to become wealthy on your own!)

> ## Whether you're an employee or on your own, the principle is the same...

So let's say you're a supervisor of five people, and you've been appropriately rewarded. If you want to expand that, if you still want more money, you're not going to get it unless you are providing more value. How can you provide more value than being a supervisor of five people? You can become a supervisor of more people. Perhaps you can become a branch manager and be over thirty people instead of just five.

By doing so, you're providing value for those thirty people, because you're now responsible for helping these thirty folks perform their tasks right so they can keep their jobs. You're overseeing their efforts and responsibilities; you're helping them earn a living, and by doing so you're providing value to thirty families. You're also providing value to your company, of course, because you're helping to ensure that the operations you oversee are running smoothly. Therefore, the value you can expect in return – the paycheck, salary or bonus you get – should be substantially more than when you were a supervisor of five people.

Do you see how it works? You can continue to get more money if you provide more value. If you influence more people, if you become responsible for helping even more people, you should be rewarded accordingly. You can even become the CEO of the company; that's what I did when I wanted more value. I had to offer more value too. Of course, we all know of newsworthy cases where the CEO of a major company didn't offer much value to the firm, and yet raked in all the rewards of that position. However, boards of directors and shareholders are becoming more unwilling to put up with CEOs who don't do their jobs.

> **...Create more value, and you can demand more reward!**

I like to think I provided a lot of value when I was a CEO. But I wasn't always a CEO; in fact, I've gone through the entire career process I outlined above. I have worked at an ordinary job where I went to the office, putting in my eight hours and then coming home – day after day, week after week, year after year – just to get a paycheck. Then I became a supervisor of five people. Then I became the person in charge of the department. Then I became the owner of the company and the CEO with 150 employees working for me. When you have that level of responsibility – when you are providing jobs for 150 families, and when it is your responsibility to make sure the company is running profitably – then you can expect a lot more value in return.

In some companies you can become wealthy by being a CEO. Indeed, I became a millionaire, and a lot of people would consider that wealth – but it still had limits that I found unsatisfying. What if you wanted to expand beyond that, as I did? It all comes down to the value that you're giving to others: the way you help other people, either by providing them with a product, or a service, or both.

I happened to be in a service company, because we were providing the service of construction coordination. We were in the field of engineering and architectural design. We worked with real estate investors and developers – entrepreneurs who found pieces of property and would come to us asking how they could turn it into millions of dollars.

Create value for millions of people to earn millions of dollars!

We would craft ideas out of our imagination regarding what the owners could do with their property. Then we would do the design and engineering, secure permits, and help the owners find contractors to construct churches, schools, office buildings, warehouses and many other types of commercial/industrial properties. In the process, we were helping people have places to live, to work, to worship or to go to school. We were helping our clients achieve their dreams and create millions of dollars for themselves. Of course we made lots of money too. Why? Because we were providing value to a lot of people.

So how do you get the kind of value you want for yourself? You do it by providing value to others. You offer your services and/or your products to the world, and you do it on the magnitude that will give you the return you want. If you want to get a lot, you have to give a lot.

Earlier I mentioned the woman who ran a private school for thirty children and wondered why she wasn't making millions of dollars. I explained to her that this was because she was only providing service to thirty people. You cannot expect thirty people to pay you millions of dollars every year of your life – that is, unless they are very wealthy people and you are selling an extremely high-priced service or product. I'm afraid that even the most exclusive private school doesn't fit that category.

Everyone has a million dollar idea, including YOU!

I told this woman that if she wanted to expand her scope and teach, say, 1,000 children, she could provide teaching via the Internet. She could set up curricula or models of school systems, and begin hiring teachers to work with her to create a nationwide school system based on the proprietary model of which she was so proud. If she does it right, she can make millions of dollars every year for the rest of her life.

Everybody has a different interest, and I believe everyone has at least one million-dollar service or product in them – maybe more. I do know this: you will be most successful, and have absolutely the most fun in your life, when you do something you love to do. Even if you don't know yet how to make money doing it, believe me, there *is* a way. (This is where you use your imagination!)

I wrote in an earlier chapter about Pat and Linda Parelli, the people who have made millions of dollars working with horses and training others how to work with horses. The Parellis had always loved working with horses. They took something that was a joy to them – a pleasure, a hobby, something fun to do – something that initially they had done for free, just because they so enjoyed doing it. Then they imagined how to turn that into a million dollar empire for themselves – an empire in which they got paid to do what they loved to do. As they became more successful they created ways to expand their enterprise and bring value to even more people. And they reaped even more value for themselves. Pat and Linda Parelli are living examples of principle number six of my Formula: *Exchange value in a big way.* If you want more money, you do it by providing more value to more people.

$$\left(\begin{array}{c}\textbf{If the act of giving}\\\textbf{is planting the seeds...}\end{array}\right)$$

The power of giving

There are two kinds of giving in the world:

1. Giving to get, with the expectation of some sort of return
2. Giving simply for the sake of giving – out of the goodness of your heart, with no expectation of return

Let's talk about the second type first. Maybe you give money to your favorite charities. Maybe you donate clothing or blankets to the homeless shelter downtown, or you give food to the local food bank. Maybe you give of your time to help out at that homeless shelter, or maybe you're the first in line to volunteer to help where you're needed when a neighboring community has been hit by a natural disaster like a hurricane, tornado or flash flood.

These are just a few examples of the ways people give without expecting to receive anything in return. Yes, I know that some people who donate to charity are motivated at least in part by the tax deductions, and some participate in publicly altruistic events such as charity balls partly (if not mostly) for the prestige and attention, and some people perform community service as part of their punishment for an offense of some sort. But countless thousands of other folks give out of the goodness of their hearts, because they feel it is the right thing to do. When you give in that manner, you receive happiness, peace and joy into your life. It has even been scientifically demonstrated that doing good makes you feel good, and it's good *for* you. (Some evolutionary biologists even say that altruism developed as a survival technique.)

> **...Happiness is the harvest.**

At any rate, when you give without reservation or expectation simply because you want to, that's when you receive happiness back. Happiness is the crop, the harvest you reap for that sort of giving.

The other type of giving is when you're giving for the sole reason and purpose of receiving a benefit in return. There is absolutely nothing wrong with that. You give of your time at work, for example, expecting to receive a paycheck in return. Sure, you may be fond of your boss and co-workers, and maybe you even love your job (lucky you!), but for the most part, you're in it for the money. Almost everybody gets up to go to work to give of their time with the complete expectation that they'll be paid for what they're doing. Most of them wouldn't do it otherwise.

As I said, there's nothing wrong with that. It is merely a process of giving and receiving, or, to return to our farming analogy, planting and sowing. A farmer plants the seed only because he has an expectation that the seed is going to grow into crops, from which he will receive a financial reward because of

his actions. He may derive some satisfaction from working with the earth and the crops, but if he's farming for a living, the main reason he plants the seed is to make money.

I believe that in order to lead a truly satisfying life, the kind of life where all of your dreams come true in a good way, you need to practice plenty of *both* kinds of giving. If you do, your happiness will increase along with your wealth.

There's a little bit of irony in the fact that even though so many people say they want to become rich, there are many who think you have to choose between wealth and happiness. So many people in the world think you can either be happy or you can be rich, but you can't be both. This misconception has long been reinforced by TV dramas about unhappy rich families, and for years before that there were numerous depressing novels about the miserable rich (*The Great Gatsby* by F. Scott Fitzgerald comes to mind). I'm here to say that you can have both wealth *and* happiness. I've had both, and I've also had one without the other – but you can have both, and many people do. In fact, the richest, happiest people in the world know a secret that a lot of folks don't seem to know: there isn't some huge divine law that says you can have one or the other, but not both. In fact, some people even believe the universe is set up in a way that you can *always* have both.

You can have both WEALTH *and* HAPPINESS by GIVING *and* RECEIVING!

How do you have both? This is where the power of giving comes in. So how do you give expecting to receive a financial reward in return, yet at the same time give just because of the happiness and joy that giving brings to your life? Here's how I do it. I've already let you know that I hire a lot of people. I hire people to mow my lawn and to trim my bushes, and I hire property managers to manage my properties. I hire people to do the maintenance on my properties. I hire construction people to do regular construction on my properties when I'm making changes to my buildings. I'm employing hundreds of people in my real estate businesses. I'm also providing places for people to live and to work in the office buildings I own.

Then there are my books. I hire people to work with me on editing my books. I work with people to do cover designs. I work with people who print my books. I pay a lot of people to help me create my books. I also pay people to warehouse and store my books, and I pay people to distribute them. I pay commissions to the stores when they sell my books. I'm therefore helping to employ the people who work in the stores, as well as the warehouse workers, the distributors who sell my books to the stores, the truck drivers who deliver my books, the printers who print my books, and the people who do the design and editing work for me on my books.

$$\left(\begin{array}{c} \textbf{HAPPY WEALTHY PEOPLE} \\ \textbf{are as willing to PAY} \\ \textbf{as they are} \\ \textbf{to BE PAID!} \end{array}\right)$$

I can approach these transactions in one of two ways. I could begrudgingly and resentfully pay all of these people for doing those things because it's the only way I can get them done. But I know that if I'm going to earn massive amounts of money, I need to take an entirely different approach to *spending* it.

Instead of being resentful, I can be glad to pay every one of these people I hire. By doing so, I get the best of both worlds. I make money through my giving, but I also enjoy giving. I enjoy knowing that I am helping people make a living. Yes, I expect

service in return... but sometimes I give even more than the contract states, and I truly enjoy that. I also get rewards from it, both tangible and intangible.

Let me give you an example. I have some yard workers who moved to the US from Guatemala – legally – some years ago. I made contact with them about five years ago and I began employing them to do different things. They can do a lot of yard and maintenance work, and when they told me what they felt their services were worth, I said, "Fine, that's what I'll pay you." Then a year later, they said they wanted a little more, so I said, "Fine, I'll pay you that." I was glad to pay them whatever they asked me to pay them (within reason, of course, and their requests *have* been reasonable so far), because I know they don't have a lot. They have a lot of work in the summer, but in the winter they hardly have any work at all, so they have to make the most of their summer jobs.

I'm glad to pay them, because I'm glad to help them out. It's almost like a charitable donation. If I'm willing to give to charity to help the poor, why would I not be willing to pay these reliable workers a great wage? I feel they are definitely earning their keep.

You'll never get millions of dollars if you begrudge spending every one!

During their work day, these workers generally take a break of about a half hour or forty-five minutes, during which time they run up to the store to buy food for themselves for lunch. They told me once that they charge me for that time. In other words, they expect that I'm going to pay them while they're away on their lunch break. I thought about it for a few moments and I told them, "Well, that's not the customary way to do it here. Normally, you get paid for the time you're working, and you don't get paid for the time you take off for a lunch break." Which is true, of course. Most workers in the U.S. don't get paid to be on their lunch break, but you know what? I like these people, and I really want to help them. So I said, "Hey, that's fine with me. You clock in at the time you get here and clock out at the time you leave for the day – and if you take a lunch break, I'll pay you for the entire day."

I'm giving generously, out of the goodness of my heart, because I want to, and it brings me great joy. And as I said, these are very hard workers, who are definitely worth what I am paying them.

I know I'm making money off the whole deal. For every hour they're working, I am saved from having to do that work. I might pay them $15 an hour, but all day long they're getting chores done that I now don't have to do, so I can work on things that create value far in excess of $15 an hour – maybe $1500 or even $15,000 an hour.

> **I gladly pay people to do work if it frees my time so I can generate more million-dollar ideas.**

With all of the ideas I'm generating, the books and talks I'm putting together, the real estate properties I'm purchasing, the financial deals I'm making at the bank – in an hour or even less I can make a decision, make a connection at a bank, or find a deal that might save me $50,000 or make me $500,000. If I have to pay $15 an hour even for some workers who are on the clock during their lunch break, that's okay – because I know that financially I am way ahead. I'm not going to bicker with them about the price. I'm not going to bicker about whether I pay them for lunch or not, because that's resisting, and I want to give. This is my way of doing both kinds of giving in order to increase my wealth and my happiness (not to mention that of other people). I always give jobs to people and pay money in a way that guarantees I'm going to make more money back. I'm also very generous in my attitude, which translates to how I react when people ask for a raise or say they want to be paid for lunch.

The more I practice giving in these ways, the richer and richer I get!

It's the same with my other enterprises. When somebody is giving me a price to print my books, for example, I could try to persuade them to lower their prices. I could put the pressure on them and get them involved in a bidding war with competitors, but that's not going to bring happiness to me. And even if they do bring their price down and I hire them, they may very well feel resentful – and justifiably so. The transaction will still bring financial reward, but it won't bring happiness to both parties. Well, I want both – financial reward and happiness. And I know it's possible to have both, because I manage to do it again and again. I've never seen that my attitude has limited my ability to make a lot of money – quite the contrary! The more I practice this sort of giving, the richer and richer I get.

Of course, I am a smart shopper. I do my homework so I always have a pretty good idea of the market value of the services I'm paying for. I'm not a walking target for price gouging, because that's not going to increase my wealth *or* my happiness. I go into a situation fully expecting to be treated fairly, and expecting to treat the other person fairly, and this has worked out very well for me, as well as for the people with whom I do business.

If I have one caveat about giving, it is this: *Be generous, but always be smart in how you give as well.* You cannot just give money away and expect you're going to get rich unless you're giving it in the right way.

A farmer doesn't just throw his seed carelessly all around the place, hoping he's going to create the crop he wants. He plants it specifically in the soil he has prepared for it, in order to get the best crop. It's the same thing with your giving. If you give all over the place – to your church, to charities, to people down the street, the Girl Scouts and Boy Scouts, the boys' and girls' clubs – that may very well make you happy, because you're giving out of the goodness of your heart. However, if you're expecting to become rich from that type of giving – if you think the Universe Genie is going to smile down upon you and say, "Hey, this is a good person; I think I'll bestow a reward of great riches!" – it just doesn't work that way.

You also need to pick and choose your "causes." You have to be prepared for the fact that once you give to one organization (unless you give anonymously), you will almost certainly be deluged not only with more requests from that same organization, but from numerous others. Some of these folks are very persistent, their pleas carefully orchestrated to tug at your heartstrings and play on your guilt.

Be generous in your giving, but be smart as well.

As a consequence, many people are either "guilted" into giving more than they are comfortable giving, or they get angry and stop giving altogether. Neither outcome leads to happiness for the giver or for the charity. The truth is that no matter how much money you have to give, you cannot save the entire world, so you might be better off just picking a few "worthy causes" at a time, refusing to let yourself be bullied into giving more than you want.

The main point to remember here is that there are two kinds of giving: the kind of giving that helps make you happy, and the kind where you expect a reward – i.e., getting rich.

When you give to the boys' and girls' clubs or to a charity, don't do it with the expectation of getting rich (again, you may be doing it partly for the tax deductions, and while those may be helpful, they will not make you rich). If you expect that charitable giving is going to make you wealthy, you have the wrong idea about how The Formula works.

Nevertheless I still promote charitable giving; I practice it myself and I hope you do, too. I want to always give like that – out of the goodness of my heart, not resentfully or begrudgingly or because someone made me feel guilty. I want to do it because it's a good thing to do and it brings me joy and helps bring happiness to others.

However, I know that type of giving doesn't bring financial reward. If I want financial reward, I also have to give in the other way. So I teach classes. I write books and I charge for those. I buy real estate and I provide places for people to live or work, but I charge them rent.

In all cases I am giving. I'm giving to the boys' and girls' clubs, and the homeless shelter, and numerous other good causes, and that makes me happy.

But if I want to get and stay rich, I also have to give value with the expectation and demand to be paid for that value. In my case, I provide value to the world through real estate and other products and services.

It's the same thing with you: When you want to become rich you must give, but you must give in the right way, with the right seed planted in the right soil, in order to get the crops you are expecting.

Continuing education

At the beginning, of this chapter, and in numerous other places in this book, I suggested you could have things like fancy cars, airplanes, vacation spots in the Bahamas, even your own private jet. *You can have all of these things if you want them.* In fact, you can have those things for free – without spending any of your own money – when you learn how to do it using my Formula. Last month I offered a free teleseminar where I taught how to purchase a brand new luxury car like a BMW or Mercedes without spending a dime of your own money.

I wasn't just teaching theory; I use this process myself. A few months ago I was in Philadelphia attending a class called "The Million Dollar Author Crash Course," put on by Steve Harrison. I'm a big believer in continual learning, and I will gladly pay for the wisdom of the best teachers who can help me be successful in my many ventures. If you're even thinking about writing a book, I highly recommend Steve Harrison's awesome course. Find out more about him on the web at www.freepublicity.com/crashcourse.

While in Philly, I was sitting in my hotel room one night and I decided that I wanted a new car. I've been driving my car for a long time and I wanted a new one. This was a perfectly understandable desire. I teach people how to make millions of dollars, I've got millions of dollars of my own, I wanted a new car and I felt I deserved a new car. The twist was that I didn't want to spend any of my own money to get it. Why? Simply because I knew I didn't have to! So I decided at that moment that I would use my Formula to get the $60,000 or $70,000 car I wanted – and I would do it without spending any of my own money.

If you want to learn the specific details of how to do that, go to my website, www.formulaforbecomingamillionaire.com, and look for my teleseminar or my book that teaches you how

to do just that. In the teleseminar I gave recently, I shared the secrets for using real estate to buy anything you want without spending a dime of your own money.

> # Learn how to buy a new car (or anything you want) without spending a dime of your own money. www.FormulaForMillionaires.com.

As soon as I got home from Philadelphia, I found some apartment buildings and got them under contract. During a three-month period, I found three different properties that I ended up purchasing for $4.5 million dollars. By buying those properties, I was now providing value to 64 families who needed a place to live. By giving that value with the expectation that I would get a financial return by way of rent paid to me, I was making enough money to have those properties now purchase the car for me.

It doesn't matter what type of vehicle or toy you want, you can easily buy whatever you desire with properties like those that I purchased, without spending a dime of your own money. Those properties would not only buy the car, but they would pay all the gas ever needed for that car. They would pay the insurance, the maintenance and the license and tag fees. They would support the cost of my car forever. As long as I owned those properties and as long as I owned that car, these properties were going to pay for everything I ever needed associated with that car – and I would never have to pay a dime of my own money.

You can do this too.

By the way, during the time I was purchasing those three properties, I was also writing this book. So I was also creating a new way to provide even more value to more people. And yes, I *am* going to buy that brand new BMW!

The one thing I didn't mention yet is that I didn't pay for that $4.5 million dollars in properties with my own money either. I used The Formula in this book to purchase them. If you want to learn more details about how I did it with real estate, go to my website and check out the next teleseminar.

Sometimes I offer these teleseminars absolutely free – you never know when it will be – so if this is something that interests you, I urge you visit my website to find out if there's a free teleseminar that will teach you how I make millions of dollars with real estate. How do you make enough money buying commercial real estate so you can acquire luxury cars – for free? I did it, and I'm getting ready to pick out and buy my new car right now.

The point is that *The Formula works*. It always has, and I guarantee you it will work for you too.

Planting a bigger crop

Most people simply don't understand this whole idea about giving value, and how you have to give value first, sometimes long before receiving any return. Farmers have always understood it. You're not going to get a crop until you plant the seed. If you want a bigger crop, plant more seed. If you want a different kind of crop, what do you do? You plant a different kind of seed. Most people understand that they go to work to make money, but as I already explained, there's a limited amount of value that you're going to get when you do that.

Some people choose to be self-employed, thinking, "I'm my own boss now. I can make more money."

Many dentists, doctors, painters and other contractors are self-employed. All of these people provide value to others, so they get a reward. Dentists or doctors in private solo practice might see eight to ten patients during the day – five or six days a week, every week, all year long – so they're providing value to a large number of people. It's the same thing with a painter or contractor who comes and works on your house, and then works on somebody else's house next week, and so forth. They're providing value to several different people. Yet these are all still very limited ways of providing value. The number of people a dentist can see in any given month or year has a limit, because a dentist is only one person.

> ## Even highly paid professionals are limited in their earnings. They won't get truly wealthy unless they work The Formula.

There is only so much time every day, week, month or year. There are only so many hours in your life, and you can only see so many people. Even for highly paid professionals such as doctors, dentists, attorneys, engineers, architects or contractors, there's only so much money they can make. Still, for the most part self-employed individuals can make more money than they could if they were working at a typical job for somebody else.

Yet they are still not going to get rich – not the kind of rich I'm talking about. And believe me, I'm talking about *very* rich. The Formula I'm teaching you in this book is not about doubling or tripling your income; it's about making your income go up ten times and then ten times again. It's not about making $100,000 a year, and it's not even about making a million dollars – it's about making millions and millions of dollars every year of your life for as long as you live.

It's about learning how to create millions and millions of dollars while you're sitting on the beach in Hawaii or the Bahamas, or while you're driving your fancy car. It's about making money while you sleep. That's what I am teaching in the principles laid out in this seven-part Formula for becoming incredibly rich.

I'm sorry to say that being self-employed will not do that for you. When you're self-employed, just as when you're working for someone else, you only get paid as long as you work.

> # Want to become *incredibly* rich? Expand, expand, EXPAND... *create more value.*

What if you own an entire company; can you get rich that way? It all depends, and if you've read this far in the chapter, you probably know that it depends on how much value you're providing to other people. If you have a product or service or maybe even information to sell, if you only sell that product or service to thirty people, or if you only give classes to thirty people, you're not going to become wealthy. You have to expand. You have to create more value.

If you can find a way to do it over the Internet, do it! Create advertising and go national or even international, traveling around to major cities giving classes and workshops – not to only thirty people, but to 300 people and then to 3,000 people and more. That's when you can begin creating real wealth for yourself. Remember, the amount of value you provide to others through your company will determine your wealth.

Let's say you've created a new machine for exercising and you want to market it, so you go door-to-door and sell it. If you're lucky, you sell perhaps fifty of those machines during the year. Unless they are extraordinarily high-priced, you're probably not going to become extremely wealthy. You might make a good living, and you might even be happy with the amount of money you're making – but you won't become incredibly wealthy. To do that, you have to provide more value to more people, not just selling door-to-door to fifty folks, but going on TV with an infomercial.

Love them or hate them, the truth is that millions of people watch these infomercials and begin buying the product, either by calling on the phone at the time they watch, or by going on-line and ordering from a web site. You can also create affiliate programs where others sell your product for you on their own web sites for a commission. They're doing a lot of your marketing for you – and if it's done right, you get wealthier, they get wealthier, and everyone is happy.

Soon you're advertising to millions of people and selling thousands of products – not just fifty units a year, but thousands a year – which is how you create wealth.

Do you see how it can all be very simple? *You get wealthy when you provide value to other people, and the more value you provide, the wealthier you will get.* If you provide value to one person, you're not going to get wealthy. If you provide value to thirty to fifty people, you might make a little more money, but you're still not going to be wealthy. If you want to get wealthy – I mean incredibly, astoundingly, eye-poppingly wealthy, you have to provide value to hundreds of thousands or even millions of people. In order to get thousands or hundreds of thousands of people to buy your product, you have to be advertising and making yourself known in any and every legitimate way you can think of. Once again, that's where your imagination comes in.

You know what you want to provide, because you have the focus and desire and you've decided what you love to do – so much so that you would do it even if you didn't get paid. Whether it's writing books, speaking, painting, singing, creating a product, working with horses, doing karaoke, or teaching children in a private school environment... only you know what you're passionate about. From there, you can craft your vision by using your imagination. You can imagine all of the ways you can create something of value to the world, and provide it on a large scale.

Now that you understand the principle of exchanging value, and now that you understand that to become rich you have to exchange value on a large scale, you can use your imagination to come up with the details of just what you need to do. Once you do that, the next step is what we talk about in the next and final chapter: taking action. Without taking action, of course, nothing will happen. But how do you begin taking action when you don't know what to do or how to do it? How do you actually take those first real steps on your own personal path to wealth when you don't even know where to start?

Well, hold on to your hat, as well as to that "impossible" wish list we talked about at the beginning of this chapter, because the last-but-certainly-not-least thing we're going to talk about is how you are going to TAKE ACTION. Without action, your dreams can never become reality. *With* it, there's no limit to what you can accomplish.

> **"The only wealth which you will keep forever is the wealth you have given away."**
> *~ Marcus Aurelius*

Desire it, imagine it, dream it, believe it.
Call on the Source,
the Higher Power,
the universe
to help you create it.

Do what you need to do within;
just remember that to make it real,
you have to ACT.

But if you've laid the groundwork,
your actions will be nearly effortless.
And you will finally be living
an extraordinary life.

STEP 7

TAKE ACTION

This chapter explains the seventh and final step in my seven-part Formula For Becoming A Millionaire: TAKE ACTION. Among other things you will learn:

    1. A simple 1-2-3 plan to get you started on your new life

    2. How "working backwards" can move you forward

This is the final principle in my seven-point Formula For Becoming A Millionaire. Like most good endings, however, this one is really just a beginning.

By now it should come as no surprise that you must take action to become a millionaire. Furthermore, you have to take *a lot of action* – and you have to start right now. Does that sound a little disappointing to you? Are you a bit disheartened by knowing that…

    1. you have to take action…

    2. you have to take a lot of it, and…

    3. you have to begin immediately if you're ever going to be wealthy?

Don't let any of this worry you. I've been honest with you all along about the fact that you can't get something for nothing.

You probably already knew that anyway, but some folks still cling to the hope that some divine magical force is going to bestow mountains of wealth upon them because they envision it, or they desire it, or they're simply good and deserving people.

As I've said before, I do believe that God or Source or the universe, or whatever higher power or greater intelligence exists, will work *with* you – but he/she/it/they won't do all of your work *for* you. So go ahead, invoke your higher power(s), but then prepare to roll up your sleeves and get busy.

> ## That "higher power" will definitely work *with* you – but won't do all the work *for* you.

The good news is you don't have to work *hard* to "get there." You don't have to suffer for success. You don't have to do anything you don't want to do. Remember, you want to be rich *and* happy – not just one or the other. In fact, the best way to become the biggest millionaire and be happy at the same time is to do it by focusing only on the things you love to do. That's the secret that so few seem to know. *I* didn't realize that secret for many years myself, even after I was already a millionaire (and working hard to be one).

Then I learned the secret of taking action without having to work hard or do a bunch of things that are less pleasant to me than having a root canal or cleaning the toilet. I learned that you or I or anyone can stop doing all the things we don't want to do and begin having real fun while making money. When I learned that secret, I quit my job, walked away from my lucrative career and started having real fun. At the same time, I began making money. A *lot* of money! You can too.

I guarantee there's a way to make mass amounts of money while having an incredibly fun time. That's what this chapter is about. It's about...

1. Taking action in a way to get where you want to go without having to work hard, and...
2. Doing it in a way that it's all fun.

Everyone thinks you have to work so hard and learn to do things you don't want to do to get rich. That's why a lot of people don't even try. Some people have told me, "Paul, I don't have time to work on getting rich. I would rather have someone else manage my money for me. I don't want to have to do all the things you're talking about – you know, all that thinking about what I want to do, and about where to put my money. I don't want to take action steps and have to plan for my life; I just want someone else to do all that."

To me this is unbelievable. I don't understand that logic, because the people who tell me they don't have time to get rich are the same people who spend an incredible amount of time struggling with the problems that result from being middle-class/poor.

They spend a lot of time doing things to save their money, as we talked about in chapters one and two. They clip coupons, and then spend hours driving around to different stores that may not be all that convenient in order to redeem those coupons. They spend their precious time off from work mowing the lawn, doing home repairs, washing the car and other chores they may not particularly enjoy, because they don't want to "waste" the money to pay someone else to do it. In other words, the poor spend their precious and irreplaceable time trying to save small amounts of money – whereas the wealthy spend their renewable money in order to save their irreplaceable time. *The rich know that time is more important than money.*

I've been straight with you all along about the fact that successfully working this Formula takes time. After all, it takes time to…

1. *think* about what you want in your life,
2. *imagine* the possibilities,
3. *cultivate* a belief in yourself that's powerful enough to spur you to action, and…
4. *begin taking action steps* to move yourself towards whatever it is you want to do, have, or be.

Curiously enough, however, the people who tell me they don't have time to do The Formula are the same folks who spend even *more* time clipping coupons, traveling across the city to find a sale rather than pay full price, or having a friend drive them to the airport so they don't have to spend money at the parking garage. These are the same people who spend months looking for the best bargain in a new car, perhaps waiting till the end of the year to get a clearance deal on last year's model.

> # Why waste time looking for bargains, when you could spend that time generating wealth so you wouldn't NEED to look for bargains?

Now, there's really nothing wrong with waiting till the end of the year for closeouts if you don't absolutely need or want a new car right now. But if you do need a new car now, and you spend most of your waking and non-working hours hunting for just the right deal, I think you're wasting your time!

Over the course of a year, countless people spend incredible amounts of time to save a few thousand dollars at most – and for some reason they feel that the time spent is well worth the money saved.

What I'm teaching here with The Formula is basically to *use that same amount of time in a totally different manner,* doing the exact opposite thing. Instead of trying to save money by using up all your time, I'm teaching you not to worry about the money. Don't love the money, feel free to spend the money – but be stingy with your time. Save your time to practice these seven principles I've been talking about, and by doing so, you can have fun, you can leave your job if you want, and you can create a new job around what you absolutely love to do.

You won't just save a few thousand dollars in a year. By spending the same amount of time focusing on this Formula as so many other people spend concentrating on saving money, you can easily *make* a million (or millions) of dollars in a year.

Therefore, when people say, "I don't have time to do all those things you teach" ...well, I don't always say this out loud, but I always think it: "You know what? You're already spending that amount of time that you tell me you don't have. You're just doing it in a way that keeps you poor."

> # Think you don't have time to work The Formula? You're ALREADY spending the time, but in a way that keeps you poor.

This book is all about doing things in a way that makes you rich. For the first several chapters, we focused more on "thinking" rich, but now we're talking about "doing" rich. So Step 7 is about taking action – and action takes a little time. That's why in Chapters 1 and 2 we talked about the need for you to create some time in your life. One point I made was that you must be willing to spend some money to hire helpers, so you have time to begin taking action in a different way than you may be used to. You need to begin practicing different behaviors that will make you wealthy rather than keeping you poor.

Have you worked hard for many years but you feel you don't have much to show for it? That's the case with many people. Do you own your own home free and clear? Do you have airplanes? Do you have fast fancy cars? Do you have all the possessions you want? Do you have that vacation home in Hawaii, Florida or the Bahamas?

> # I have the freedom to make MILLIONS doing what I love to do. You can have that freedom too.

At some point you may ask if those things are even important. I said at the very beginning of this book that acquiring material "stuff" is not the way to happiness. You can have all the newest and most expensive toys in the world and still be miserable. Still, there's no denying that if you already have a solid foundation of happiness – good relationships, good health and the like – some of these material things can add immeasurably to your joy in life. In the end, only you can answer the question, "Are these things important?" If you desire them, then yes, they are important – to you.

I know it was important for me to have a lot of these things. They're certainly not the most important parts of my life. Freedom and happiness and the relationships in my life are the most important to me, but beyond that, I do want vacation homes in beautiful places like Hawaii. I do want the freedom to be able to walk away from my career and do the types of things I love to do – and not have to worry about where the money is going to come from.

I want to have the freedom that comes from knowing I can create millions of dollars doing the things I want to do. I want to have the financial freedom to go do all the fun things I want to do – whether I'm bringing value to other people or just kicking back and playing.

Do you have that freedom?

Some people tell me, "Paul, I love my job." Do you really? Here's a test: If you stopped being paid, how long would you continue to go to work every day? Some of you might very well say you would continue to work. So maybe you *do* love your job – and if you do, I congratulate you, because that is your passion.

> **Even if you really love your job, you could take the passion & energy you bring to your work – and make far more money on your own!**

But I still would urge you to consider that maybe, just maybe, you could take that passion and make scads more money than you're making at your current job.

Earlier in this book I mentioned a three-day event I attended in New York, where I had the opportunity to meet with over 100 national TV producers. As I told you, I got the chance to meet them face-to-face for three days and speak with each of them individually. I pitched my ideas about what we could do on their TV shows, and they gave me feedback. We talked about what they were most interested in, what I have to offer and how I could better pitch them in a month or two when they might be doing a show that would fit well with my ideas.

It was a great experience. I was with Steve Harrison's group, the National Publicity Summit. I mentioned Steve in the previous chapter, and I want to reiterate that I highly recommend his classes, courses and events if you're interested in being an author, getting on television or learning how to get in touch with national TV producers.

In the evenings, attendees got to socialize with each other. One of the women in our group was Donna Krech, creator and founder of a brilliant weight-loss and health system called Thin & Healthy's Total Solution (http://www.thinandhealthy.com). Donna shared some things she had learned through her work as a personal development coach and an author. She said that one of the things she'd found was that all people have within themselves a gift – something they're particularly good at doing. This gift is something nobody has had to teach them how to do; it's something they were born with. It is the thing they were born to do.

That really resonated with me. I agree with her that we all have a special gift, and I would take this thought a step further and say that virtually everybody's gift can be transformed into a million-dollar idea. When you figure out what your own gift is, you should pursue it as your passion, because it is the very thing that will bring you the most happiness. It is also that thing that you would do even if you weren't getting paid. When you apply The Formula that I'm teaching through this course to that thing you're most passionate about, *that's* when you will begin making the most money you can possibly make – for the very reason that you *are* passionate about it, and you would do it even if it weren't for the money.

What's your "one thing?"

Maybe you're saying, "Okay, great… I want that passion, and it sure would be wonderful to make money doing something I'm passionate about, but the truth is, I don't know what that is. How do I figure out what it is, Paul?"

You may remember a scene in the 1991 movie, *City Slickers*, where Billy Crystal's character Mitch is having a conversation with Curly, played by the late Jack Palance. Curly asks Mitch, "Do you know what the secret of life is?" He holds up one finger and answers his own question: "This."

Mitch, ever the smart-aleck, asks, "Your finger?"

Ignoring that, Curly continues, "One thing. Just one thing…"

Mitch asks, "But, what is the 'one thing?'"

Curly smiles and says, "That's what *you* have to find out."

That may sound like a cop-out, the kind of advice that makes you want to say, "Hey, thanks for nothing." But Curly has a point (so to speak). Nobody can answer life's most important questions for you. I like to think I am providing some good guidelines here, along with a little inspiration and motivation by sharing some real-world examples, but in the end, you are the one who is going to have to answer your most important questions.

What would you do if you had all the money you ever wanted? You can do it now!

It takes a little time and effort – and, yes, action – to think about it, to imagine it and to ponder what it is in your life that you love to do most. In my opinion, this is one of the most important things you can do. Yet so many of us are so busy getting up and taking the action of just going to work every day to collect a paycheck, that we don't take time out – ever – to think about what we wish we could do with our time instead.

If it weren't for the money, what would you do? After you make your millions and millions of dollars and you don't need any more money, after you've traveled around the globe going to all the exotic places you've always dreamed of, what would you do then? What would you do, or continue to do, when the time comes that money isn't that exciting to you anymore? I know that's hard to imagine now, but I guarantee you that time will come. When you make millions and millions of dollars, and continue to do so, it's like anything else: after a while you just get used to it.

What will energize you once the excitement of being a millionaire has worn off? THAT'S your passion.

Ask anybody who's been in that position for a long time, and they'll tell you that's the way it is. It will happen to you, too; I guarantee it. You will make millions of dollars, and eventually, after a few years, you'll get used to it. The question is: When that time comes – when you've acquired most or all of the toys you've longed for, when you're tired of playing golf and going to resorts or going on adventure tours on the other side of the world – what will you want to do with your time?

What is it that you want to do with your life that will bring value to *you* as well as others? What would you make every effort to continue to do, whether you were rich or poor? That's what you have to figure out. That's the thing Donna Krech was speaking about when I was in New York. And I imagine that's what Curly was talking about in *City Slickers*. You have to discover, or perhaps rediscover, that thing you're passionate about, that "one thing" that's inside you that has always been there and never goes away. It may have been years since you've taken time to even think about it...but it's still there, waiting.

Maybe you're one of the lucky ones. Perhaps you've known what your passion is for a long time, and maybe you're living your life accordingly. Or maybe you just started seriously thinking about the issue as you were reading one of the earlier chapters in this book. It could be that my prompting you to change your thinking and imagine the possibilities got some ideas flowing. If so, you're a few steps ahead of many people.

The truth is that we get so busy with our jobs, families and financial responsibilities that we don't often take the time to ask ourselves the questions that need to be asked in order for us to find our passion. I want you to take that time.

"If I were God..."

Ask yourself this question: "If I were God, how would I craft my life to be perfect?" That's the thing I'm challenging you to do now, because within you there is a power bigger than yourself. Within you, there's something you can connect with, that's bigger than all of us put together – something almost divine.

> **Within you there is a power bigger than yourself... bigger than all of us put together.**

Within you is the ability to imagine incredible things, and when you believe those things can become true – and are brave enough to take action to move yourself towards those things – the incredible happens. That's what makes millionaires and billionaires. It makes the happiest people in the world. It makes the winners in life, the Olympic gold medallists, and the entrepreneurs who hit it bigger than everybody else.

That's the kind of success and happiness you can have when you put these seven steps together, applying them toward that "one thing" you were meant to do. As much as you've tried to think positive and visualize a better future for yourself, maybe it hasn't worked. So many people visualize what they want. They meditate on it and believe it's going to come, yet it never comes. Why doesn't it come? It's because they don't apply this final principle – Step 7 – that says *you have to take action, you have to take a lot of action and you have to start right now.*

It's not just about imagining and believing it; it's about doing it. More importantly, it's about creating it. *We are made to create.* We have creative ability within us. Everything that's been created in the world has been created through the imagination people have and the actions they have taken.

All the people who create wealth for themselves do the same thing:

1. They imagine it.
2. They figure out how they're going to do it.
3. They believe they have within themselves the ability to bring it about.
4. They begin taking action to move themselves towards it.

Does that sound like a lot of hard work? It did to me too at one time, but it doesn't have to be that way. I've built businesses and, as I've mentioned, I owned a company when I was only 27 years old. In the beginning, we had about forty employees, and I worked to create wealth for myself. I grew that company from having forty employees to 150 employees. I had five full-time bookkeepers doing all the accounting work just to keep up. I had three full-time technology staff members who were keeping 150 computer systems running, managing all the software and hardware interactions, working over the Internet and dealing with clients.

> # You can make money the hard way or the easy way. The Formula is the easy way.

We helped hundreds of clients every single year to create wealth for themselves through the development of over a billion dollars of real estate annually. It was a multi-million dollar business. It was a huge undertaking and a lot of work. As I described in an earlier chapter, I was so busy I didn't have time to sleep. I didn't have time to eat healthy, to exercise, to have fun or spend time with my family. I never had time to take out for myself – not even a little relaxing break, to be able to dream dreams and create visions in my mind about what I really wanted for my life.

Sure, I made money. I was a millionaire; that company was how I made my first million. But was it worth it? In retrospect, probably not. But at the time, I didn't fully understand the secret of Step 7: the principle of taking action, but not just any action. Even as I didn't fully understand Step 5 – belief – as evidenced by the fact that I was laboring under a lot of *false* beliefs, I didn't understand the principle about action. I absolutely *was* taking action to grow my company. In fact, I was using all of the principles in The Formula to create wealth for and through my company, but *I was doing it in a way that failed to make me happy.* I wasn't taking action in a way that would bring peace and happiness to me as well as wealth.

> **I worked so hard for so many years because I thought I had to. I didn't understand The Formula.**

The point I want to make is that the action you take can be fun, and it doesn't have to be hard work at all. I learned this later in my life and career when I discovered that my Formula worked, even without hard work, even doing only the things I loved to do. In fact, it worked better *without* hard work and without my having to do things I disliked. Learning this was a breakthrough. It was then that I decided to walk away from that multi-million dollar career with the trust and belief that I could take this Formula, apply it to anything and make mass amounts of wealth. I was determined to walk away from a corporate career and apply this Formula to something that was strictly fun for me. To me, this included public speaking, going on the radio, writing books, traveling, going on vacation and having lots of fun.

I believed that I would take a couple of years setting this up, figuring out how it worked, getting to know and meeting important people I wanted to meet, writing a couple of books, and learning all I needed to know about advertising and marketing. That might not be your idea of a high old time, but it was (and is) all fun to me, because these were all things that I wanted to do. I believed that after a couple of years, things would finally take off in an incredibly big way... but it turned out to be even better than I had imagined.

> # I could have gone anywhere with that business. But I walked away from it because I believed in my Formula.

As I shared in an earlier chapter, I made much more money during just the first six months on my own than I would have made in the entire year as a CEO. As CEO, I made an incredible amount of money, more than most people would imagine. I told you that a lot of people thought I was crazy for walking away from that career when I had a whole future ahead of me, and I wasn't even forty years old yet. I could have gone anywhere with that business. I could have done a lot of things and made a lot of money.

But I walked away, because I believed in my Formula.

Within six months, I was already making a lot more money just in the process of setting up a new direction for my life, and getting my new businesses off the ground, than I had originally thought I would be making after a couple of years. The purpose of making this point numerous times throughout these pages is not to brag about my accomplishments or to beat you over the head with my own success story. I've told this story in multiple chapters for one reason: I felt it was important to frame my own story around several different principles in my Formula. In this way, I can illustrate an ongoing real-world example of The Formula at work. And by doing that, I hope I can encourage you to believe that you can accomplish the same in your life.

I'm far from the only person having fun and making wealth at the same time. Let me share another story – well, three stories, to be exact.

Peak experiences

Some of my favorite "home-grown" success stories involve some guys from my neck of the woods, the beautiful Pacific Northwest. One of them, Lute Jerstad, was actually from Oregon, and the other two were from my home state of Washington. Lute went to my father's high school and was a few years ahead of him in school. My dad liked mountain climbing, and Lute liked it too, but my father's mountain climbing was limited to the Pacific Northwest area. Not that this is anything to sneeze at; this area boasts some breathtakingly beautiful and challenging peaks.

(**Find your Everest and CLIMB IT!**)

Lute had much bigger dreams, though. In the early 1960s, Lute was working summers as a mountain guide on Washington's Mount Rainier while teaching drama at the University of Oregon. His life changed when he was invited to go on an expedition to the summit of Mount Everest in the Himalayas, which at 29,028 feet is the highest spot on earth. At that time, no Americans had yet reached that lofty point.

The other two fellows in this story are twin brothers, Lou and Jim Whittaker. Born in Seattle in 1929, the two were inseparable. They began mountain climbing at an early age, and first scaled Mount Rainier when they were only sixteen years old. Climbing was their passion. In 1951, the Whittakers were recruited to be guides on Mount Rainier by an international ski racer named Bill Dunaway, who ran the guide service there. The following year, the Whittaker twins took over the service.

There really wasn't a lot of money in it, and at the close of the 1955 season, the Whittakers left Rainier for higher paying full-time jobs in the outdoor equipment business. Lou joined Osborn & Ulland, and Jim went to work for Recreational Equipment, Inc. (REI, which had been founded as a co-op in 1938), as its first full-time employee. Both brothers continued to climb mountains, however, often taking paying clients with them.

They were still pretty much inseparable, but their lives diverged in 1963 when Jim Whittaker went with the American expedition to Mount Everest. Lou was invited to be on that expedition, but stayed behind to open his own sporting goods store, which he called Whittaker's Chalet.

> # Your BIGGEST REGRETS in life
> ## will be the things you
> ## *wanted* to do,
> ## but *didn't*.

On May 1, 1963, Jim Whittaker became the first American to reach the summit of Mount Everest. He and his Sherpa guide had run out of oxygen but still managed to make it to their goal, and Whittaker planted an American flag on the highest point on the planet. Three weeks later, on May 22, Lute Jerstad and another man named Barry Bishop repeated the feat. Lute was the first person in the world to take movie film from the summit of Everest.

Jim Whittaker became world famous for being the first American to reach the summit of Everest, and when he came home he went on to many more adventures. In 1965, he guided Robert Kennedy up the newly-named Mount Kennedy in the Yukon. Mount Kennedy had been named in honor of Robert Kennedy's brother, the late US President John F. Kennedy, who had been assassinated exactly six months to the day after Lute

Jerstad had reached the summit of Everest. Jim Whittaker also led the 1990 Everest Peace Climb that brought together climbers from the US, USSR and China. Besides taking more than a dozen climbers on the summit, the expedition hauled off a large amount of garbage left on the mountain by previous expeditions. Jim continued to work for REI as well, and in the late 1960s became the company's CEO. More recently he was named Chairman of the Board of Magellan Navigation, a company that produces handheld global positioning system (GPS) units. He is also an author and motivational speaker.

Lute Jerstad was never as famous as Jim Whittaker, but according to Austrian Norman Dyhrenfurth, who was the leader of the 1963 expedition, the achievements of Lute and some of his climbing buddies were in reality even more amazing. Lute and three other members of the team were forced to spend the night in the open just below the summit of Everest, and their mere survival in those brutal conditions was actually the most outstanding climbing feat of its day.

Like Jim Whittaker, Lute also continued to indulge his passion for climbing when he came home. He continued to teach, but that wasn't where his heart was, and he finally left academia in 1970 to begin a career in the adventure travel business. His company, Lute Jerstad Adventures, specialized in trips to India and Nepal, as well as river rafting in Oregon. Lute spent the rest of his life splitting his time between Oregon and the Himalayas. One of his pet causes was working to convince governments and local residents to set aside parts of mountain ranges as national parks.

In 1998, at the age of 62, he was leading a nine-member trekking team up 15,000-foot Mount Kalapatar in Nepal. Lute was 500 feet below the summit when he suffered a fatal heart attack. Even though his life was cut short, he died doing what he loved best. I know that's kind of a cliché, but really, how many people can make that same claim?

Not many! Thomas Hornbein, another member of the 1963 Everest expedition, said of Lute, "He was a guy who lived a life where adventure was part of his diet."

What about the other Whittaker brother, Lou? Even though he didn't climb Everest with his two buddies, he too found a way to become wealthy from his passion. His store, Whittaker's Chalet, was successful enough that he opened a second branch in Tacoma, Washington in 1967. But selling equipment proved to be less fun for Lou than climbing mountains, and by the late 1960s he was getting pretty restless.

> ## Turn your passion into profit, and you just might become another great American success story.

It so happened that the popularity of guided trips up Rainier was growing, partly because of Lou's brother Jim having conquered Everest. By 1968, the Rainier guide service was being run by John and Evelyn Anderson, who were subcontracted by the Rainier National Park Company. The Andersons didn't have much experience with guided mountain climbs, so they hired Lou to manage their summer operation and act as chief guide. When the Andersons decided they just didn't want to be in the business any longer, they sold it to Lou and his partner Jerry Lynch, an attorney friend who had helped Lou set up Whittaker's Chalet. Whittaker and Lynch bought the Andersons' entire inventory of boots, crampons, sleeping bags, ropes and other climbing equipment for $3,000.

Lou and Jerry formed Rainier Mountaineering Inc. (RMI) in late 1968, with Jerry as president and Lou – at nearly forty years of age – as vice president. Their timing was right, because in 1969, their first summer in business, interest in mountain climbing was really surging. RMI is still a very profitable business, and besides Mount Rainier, the company now leads expeditions all over the world, from Mount McKinley in Alaska to Kilimanjaro in Africa.

And Lou Whittaker? He was still joyfully climbing Rainier into his 70s, and has reached the summit over 250 times. He has made a very handsome living not only from his guide service, but from the hotel and coffee shop he owns in the vicinity of Mount Rainier National Park. Like his brother Jim, he's also a published author. As an October 2007 article in the *Tacoma Tribune News* put it, "Whittaker, it seems, is the only person in Mount Rainier's history who went to the mountaintop and found gold."

All three of these men – Lute Jerstad and Jim and Lou Whittaker – found creative ways to turn a lifelong passion into profit. Even when they weren't making much money at it, they were climbing mountains. They would have continued to climb mountains even if they had never made *any* money doing that. But they kept on doing what they loved the most. Each man in his own way, perhaps without realizing it, was using The Formula. And each in his own way became an American success story.

You can be one too.

Three steps to your future

We've established that you're not going to get where you want to go without taking action. It takes a lot of planning and effort, but it doesn't have to be hard work – not when you apply it to that one thing you're most passionate about. When I built a multi-million dollar corporation, a business with 150 people, that *was* a lot of work, because it wasn't something I was passionate about. It wasn't something I would have done for free. I did it because I got paid.

I knew I could make a lot of money doing it, and I didn't *mind* doing it; I just didn't love it. I never hated my job; in fact,

I always said I liked my job, but when it came right down to it, it wasn't a job I would have done for free if given the choice. Most people are working at jobs they wouldn't continue to do for free. So the question I want to ask you is this: If you haven't already taken time out of your busy life to think about what you truly want to do, *when* are you going to do it? When will you discover what you're passionate about, so you can begin applying these principles towards that thing you want to do most in your life?

> # Can you count to three?
> # Then you can create.
> # an action plan for yourself.

And once you have determined your passion, *how* do you begin taking action? That's a good question. A lot of people say, "I don't know! I don't even know what the first steps are." Even when you figure out what you want to do, where do you start? How do you go from being a person who has no money and not a lot of ideas about what to do, to someone who is incredibly wealthy? How do you get from where you are now to where you wish you could be in the future?

Let's not make it more complicated than it needs to be. It's as simple as one, two, three. If you can count to three, then you can create an action plan for yourself:

Step 1 calls for you to think about where you are right now. When you take any journey, it only makes sense to consult a map. But even the best maps won't do you any good until you establish your starting point, the place where the journey begins. Maybe you don't have any money and maybe you don't have a lot of education about business or advertising, but you know that where you are right now is *not* where you want to be.

So step one is about being really clear and honest with yourself about your life as you're living it right now.

Step 2 is getting clear on what you really want and where you want to go. It's like finding your destination on the road map. You know where your starting point is; now you have to pinpoint your desired destination. Put simply, you know you want to be wealthy, while doing whatever it is you're passionate about.

Step 3 involves making "the plan": deciding just what you have to do to get from where you are now to where you want to go. At first, you might not know exactly what that *"what"* is, but if you take some time and think about it every day, meditate and imagine the possibilities, and imagine what those steps might be, that will lead you to create the plan.

> # Get started NOW.
> # Don't wait till you have all
> # of the correct information,
> # or you'll never start!

You might say, "I'm not certain," but you never have to be certain! When you begin putting together a plan, put together ten steps of how to get from where you are now to where you want to be. I'm suggesting ten steps because that's a reasonable number of steps for most people. With a little effort you can easily imagine ten steps you might take. It's just like looking at the road map and deciding which roads will be best to get you to your destination.

Of those ten steps you came up with, perhaps only 50% of them might turn out to be correct, but that's okay. So I repeat: The only way to get from where you are now to where you want to be is to put together ten steps. And start going right now, *even when you know those ten steps aren't 100% accurate, even when you know that not every one of those ten steps is going to help get you where you want to be.* Do the best you can do with the information you have at the time – and you might just surprise yourself.

But you have to get started. Waiting to act until you have all the correct information is like waiting to buy a computer until the best one comes along. In both cases, you'll end up waiting forever, and you will never get what you want.

> # Hit a brick wall?
> # Take a "time out."
> # Just don't use that as an excuse
> # for prolonged inaction.

Let's look more closely at the way it works. You put together ten steps and you start going down that path. You know you have to do step number one, so you do. You know you have to do step number two, so you begin it, and then perhaps you hit a brick wall and you can't figure out how to get past it. *That's okay.* It's a normal part of the process, so you stop and re-evaluate it.

Say to yourself: "Where am I right now, and where do I want to go? What are more ideas I could imagine? No matter how impossible they seem at the time, I'm going to pretend, make believe, make up steps…and I'm going to imagine what the steps could be right now to get me from where I am to where I want to be." In other words, when you hit a brick wall, take a "time out," maybe for a day, a week or even a couple of months. You refine and reformulate your plan, using your imagination to figure out new ideas – and then you go on.

One caveat, though: Don't take too long refining and reformulating. Don't use that "brick wall" as an excuse for prolonged inaction!

So let's say you get step two figured out, and then take steps three or four, and perhaps you hit a brick wall again, and your plan simply is not working. It's a dead end, and you know the path you set out on isn't correct, and it's not getting you where you want to go. But that's okay, it's still part of the process. That's the only way you're going to make progress. Look at it this way: if you're at step five, you're halfway there.

And so what if you've made a mistake or two along the way? I have learned that, with very few exceptions, the people who get what they want out of life aren't afraid of making mistakes. They're not afraid to start going, even if they know there's a chance that the direction they're going is the wrong direction. Most people never get anywhere in life because they're afraid to move, and as a result, they don't even take the first steps. Most people say, "I don't know what steps to take, so I'm not going to take *any* steps." The people who get somewhere say the opposite. They say, "I'm not sure what steps to take, but I'm going to imagine some and I'm going to start taking them."

They say, "I know along the way I'm going to hit some brick walls, and I'll have to stop; maybe I'll have to turn around 180 degrees and go back the other way, but that's okay. It's better that I'm taking steps and moving than not moving at all, because most people *don't* move at all."

> # The people who get what they want out of life aren't afraid of making mistakes.

The people who are the most successful *have* moved. They've made mistakes, and then they've turned around and fixed their mistakes. When they hit a brick wall, they create a new plan. That new plan takes them a few more steps, then maybe they hit a brick wall again. They have to make yet another new plan, *but they keep on*. They're persistent and they're not afraid of taking steps, even when they know some of those steps are going to be missteps. They have learned that the only way to figure out how to fix the steps that don't work is to begin actually taking them.

If you're uneasy about heading off in a direction that you know might be the wrong one, just be assured that when you get to that brick wall, you *will* know what to do.

Working backwards to move forward

About 100 years ago, Henry Ford was considered one of the wealthiest men in America. When he was being interviewed by Napoleon Hill for the book *Think and Grow Rich*, Hill asked him, "What is the characteristic to which you credit your biggest success?" One of the things Ford said (I'm paraphrasing, but the point is pretty clear) was that he was not afraid to start heading down the path, even when he knew he was going to run into some obstacles.

Most people never begin heading down that path, because they're afraid of the obstacle.

Ford told Hill that it was like having to cross through a forest, knowing there is a river in the middle with no way across. Most people wouldn't even begin going through the forest, because they know the river is there and they don't have a plan to get across. So they don't even start on the journey. Henry Ford said he attributed his success to the fact that he *always* started the journey, even if it was just with the small steps that he knew how to accomplish. He didn't get sidetracked by the things he didn't yet know how to do. He knew he would invariably have to face those things at some point, but he also knew from experience that when he would get to that point, it would usually all work out by itself. He added that as you start going through that forest, by the time you come to the river, more times than not, you find the river has dried up and you can walk across on dry ground.

That's what we're talking about in this book. You create an action plan of how you're going to get from where you are now to where you want to be, and you use all the principles we've talked about. You have a clear and focused desire as to what you want, and you begin to imagine the possibilities. When you allow yourself to imagine the possibilities, you also free up your ability to imagine just what you're going to do to get there.

> # Don't get sidetracked by obstacles – real or imaginary!

You do it in a way that brings value to a lot of other people. That part has to be there if you're going to get wealthy. You believe that you have the power within yourself to make your dream happen. You believe in yourself, because you're not waiting for somebody to hand it to you. You're not waiting to have a lucky break in life. You're not waiting to win the lottery. You're not waiting for *anything*.

You know you have the ability within yourself to make this thing happen, because you've imagined it – and now you're going to go out and take action to begin building it.

This is what every successful person does. That's how entrepreneurs make millions of dollars. That's how the most successful people you see on television, or that you read about on Forbes.com, have done it. But you have to start somewhere. You have to create a plan for yourself.

So what can you do to put a plan together? After you've decided just what it is you want, how do you begin? Sometimes it's hard even coming up with the first step. I'll tell you what I did. When I started on my new career and walked away from being a CEO, I said, "Here's what I want. I want to be a celebrity author. I want to be known nationally across the country for my books, my speaking and my teaching. I want to be a life coach and a personal development trainer. I want to be popular. And I want to make millions of dollars."

I didn't know anything about writing or speaking. Nobody knew me nationally, and I had no connections in television, radio or the media at all. It was a new field for me. I had never had any experience in it before, so I knew where I was – which was step number one, in the 1-2-3 list above. In short, when it came to being a celebrity author, *I had nothing and I knew nothing*.

So I was clear about where I was and where I wanted to be.

> # Blocked because you can't even imagine the *first* step? No problem! Take the *last* step and work backwards.

The big question was: *Where do I begin when I'm not sure exactly what step number one should be?* Here's a trick I discovered: start by working backwards. I have found that in many cases it's easier to list the steps backwards than it is to figure out the steps going forward. In my case, I knew I number ten: I would be a celebrity author, speaker and coach. That was "where" I wanted to be. So if that was step number ten, what had to happen just before that? What would be step number nine, the step that would lead me directly into achieving step number ten?

Are you beginning to see how it works? You go backwards, imagining what has to happen to get you to that ultimate goal. And you keep going backwards until you get to where you are right now. I knew that for an author to become a nationally known celebrity, he has to be on national TV. It's the only way to get that national recognition, status or fame. So step number nine would be to get on national TV. If step number nine is getting on national TV, what has to happen before that?

What would it take for somebody to be able to get on national TV? I believed that if I could get a lot of local TV experience in many of the big cities around the country – step eight – and if I was also doing national radio – steps seven – then I could probably gain the level of renown needed to pitch my stories and ideas to the network TV producers.

What has to happen before you can get on local TV or national radio? Maybe you have to get on local radio – step number six. I figured that if I could get on local radio in my area, and do a lot of it, I could start doing local radio shows around the entire country, and eventually get onto national radio – and then on local TV stations.

What has to happen just before you get on local radio? You need to know a local radio host. That's step number five.

What would have to happen just before that? Well, you might have to meet somebody, perhaps a coach who could train you in media – and that training would be step four. How are you going to find such a person? That would be step three. You have to go to the events those people attend. And that's step two: looking for the right coach or coaches. That brings us back to step number one, which is to actually decide that you're going to go looking for a radio coach.

It's as simple as that.

Those were the steps I laid out for myself. First I had to admit (at least to myself) that I knew absolutely nothing about anything to do with radio, TV, being a celebrity, being a writer or an author. Nevertheless I put together a plan to become a nationally recognized celebrity author on national television.

Do you see how working it backwards made the process much easier?

Naturally you're probably going to want to ask me, "Well, Paul, is that the way it worked out?" For the most part, it did. Some of it changed along the way. In fact I started out looking for a local radio host and I went to an event and found one, Dr. Pat Baccili, who does the *Dr. Pat Show* here in Seattle. I mentioned Dr. Pat in my Introduction. She also happens to be a coach, and she coached me in radio and other media, so I was able to kill two birds with one host.

Once I began putting together this plan, I dared to imagine the possibilities, and I dared to believe I could make it happen. I made the decision to find a radio coach – step one. I took action by finding Dr. Pat, hiring her to train me in media and radio. I dared to take the next step and go on her show – and it worked out so well that we did lots more shows. That led to meeting other PR people, who put me on more and more radio shows. You see how it started and just went on from there.

> ## I hit brick walls but I kept going. A few months later I was in New York meeting with national TV producers.

Eventually along the way, of course, some things happened that didn't work as I had initially planned. I hit brick walls. I had to revise my plan and modify the steps, but I kept going and a few months later, I was in New York meeting with those national TV producers – which put me already at step nine. That's how it works. But you have to begin by imagining a plan and knowing that it's okay if it's not 100% correct to start with, and that you'll make some missteps along the way.

This is the process that millionaires and billionaires use to create their wealth. This is how you become free from having to go to work every day. These principles – these seven steps – will put you into the position where you can make more money while you sleep and while you're on vacation than you ever made before, no matter how smart you were or how hard you worked. By applying these principles, you can achieve the incredible wealth you desire. You can own fancy cars and airplanes, take dream vacations, own vacation homes in Hawaii and the Bahamas, have fancy yachts...the whole package.

When you have all those things, eventually you'll realize money isn't all that important. And you'll learn the *real* secret: that the most valuable possession you now own is the belief you have in yourself, and the knowledge that you can create anything you want for yourself, any time you want. You'll find that you use The Formula to create not only wealth, but the freedom and happiness you truly want.

And *that's* what the real secret is all about.

* * * * *

I hope by now you have a pretty good understanding of the seven principles that make up my Formula For Becoming A Millionaire (or a billionaire)! As I said at the opening of this chapter, although Step 7 is the final principle in the seven-part Formula, in reality it is only the beginning.

And I truly hope it will be a glorious new beginning for you. I know beyond a doubt that anyone can become wealthy *and* happy by diligently applying these seven principles. I wish you wealth, health and happiness beyond anything you may have ever dreamed was possible.

> # Use The Formula to create not only wealth but the freedom and happiness you truly desire.

*You feel the warm golden sun
and the balmy sea breeze on your skin...
and you close your eyes and sigh.*

*This splendid beach is a world away ~
and not just in distance ~
from the windowless office
where you once spent your days.*

*You smile, knowing
that office is now part of your past.
Money is flowing into your life ~
more money than you've ever had before.
You're providing value to the world,
and the world is giving you
dazzling gifts in return.*

And life is good.

AFTERWORD

The Adventure Is Just BEGINNING!

I hope you've had as good a time learning the seven principles of my Formula For Becoming A Millionaire as I've had writing about them. I realize that a lot of things I've said may ruffle your feathers, maybe even offend you. That's good, because if you keep thinking as you thought in the past, and keep doing the same comfortable things you have always done, your financial future is going to be the same as it was in the past. If you want to change your future to become more abundant, then I need to shake you up with the truth about money. It might shock you and even offend you because it flies in the face of everything you've been taught. But that's a good thing! And I trust that if you've made it this far in the book, you won't stop now. I look forward to working with you more through my CDs, my teleseminars, my FREE reports and through all the other ways I share this incredible Formula.

The one thought I want to leave you with is that all of those images I've been feeding you throughout these pages – you know, the fancy cars, the vacation homes, the private jets, the beautiful beaches – are not just empty words. The scenario on the facing page – of you lying on that glorious beach, smiling because you know the money is flowing in, and you're finally happy, and life is good – is not just an empty promise. That *can* be your reality, if that's what you want. And it could very well be easier – and lots more fun – than you ever dreamed.

Even more important than the fancy cars and the lovely beaches and all that money, however, is the knowledge that you have created, and are living, an extraordinary life – a life in which you are not only providing value to the world, but to yourself and your loved ones.

As you progress on your road to wealth and happiness, I want to hear from you. I want to hear about your successes, your frustrations, your triumphs. You can write to me at the address in the front of this book, or send me an e-mail at Paul@miraclewriters.com.

And again, I invite you to visit my web site,. www.FormulaForMillionaires.com. I am building an online community where you can get together with like-minded entrepreneurs, millionaires and millionaires in the making. I'm working to make this a very rewarding experience for all of us.

Thank you for joining me on this journey...and I hope you'll stay with me, because I have a lot more in store for you (browse the next few pages, and you'll get a good idea of what I'm talking about).

The fun is just beginning!

Yours in prosperity,
Paul McCormick

Meet The AUTHOR

Paul McCormick began his career working with multi-millionaire investors and entrepreneurs and soon discovered something amazing: there is a formula to becoming a millionaire, and all the wealthiest people use it. No one has ever spoken about this "Formula" – until now.

Paul used The Formula to become the owner of a multi-million dollar company at age twenty-seven and CEO by twenty-nine. But while in his thirties Paul walked away from his career, realizing jobs are not needed to create massive amounts of money.

In this book, Paul shares the 7-Step Formula For Becoming A Millionaire and tells you exactly how to make millions and millions of dollars doing only what you love doing.

Paul was certainly not born into money. His parents and grandparent knew nothing about money, other than how to work at jobs, collect a paycheck and spend it, just like most people do.

Paul is proud of his family's blue-collar, working-class background and the wonderful experiences it offered him, the skills he learned, the value of work it taught him, and the perspective he gained of people in that position. While he acknowledges that having no money is nothing to be ashamed of, he also knows that having wealth is nothing to be ashamed of, either. And we all have the choice to decide which life we want.

Once dirt poor, eating corn flakes with water and driving a 24 year-old Toyota that broke down regularly, Paul knew there had to be a better way, and set himself on the path to find it. Over many years, he constantly sought the knowledge of those who appeared to know something different from everyone else about wealth. His search brought him in contact with hundreds of wealthy entrepreneurs, and he discovered that although each had a different "story," there was a common element to virtually all of their successes – an amazing Formula for achieving wealth.

Once he figured out The Formula and applied it to his own life, the results amazed him. He no longer works at jobs he hates, and is financially free, beyond even his earlier dreams. He gets up every day and says it's like those days when you wake up wishing you didn't have to go to work, only to realize that it is Saturday and you don't.

Every day of his life is a Saturday now – not the kind where he sits around in his pajamas all day, but rather the kind where he has fun doing what he loves to do, and amassing incredible wealth doing it. Having created a way to get paid to have fun, he now spends his time teaching others how to do the same.

FREE BONUS GIFTS!

Visit
www.FormulaForMillionaires.com

To help you become a millionaire
I'm offering you some
FREE Bonus Gifts.

✦ FREE reports
✦ FREE audio downloads
✦ FREE video downloads

I want to give you as much free information
as possible, so you have the tools you need to
become financially free as I did.
Glance at the next few pages
to see the benefits you'll receive
by downloading these FREE bonus items.

I urge you now to go to
www.FormulaForMillionaires.com
You will have instant access to the FREE
videos, audios, and reports.

Sincerely,
Paul

Free Bonus #1

Formula For Millionaires
REPORT #1

The Shocking Things We Do
That *Stop Us From Being Rich*

Want to know a secret...
the simple things that keep us poor?
If I showed you 10 things you do every day
that keep you poor...
would you stop doing them?

FIND OUT NOW!

Download My FREE Report
www.FormulaForMillionaires.com

Free Bonus #2

Formula For Millionaires
REPORT #2

Lifestyle of the Affluent ~ Shocking Secrets That *Make Them Rich*

Want to know how the rich get rich?
If I showed you 3 things to do every day
that the rich do
that makes them rich...
Would you begin doing them?

FIND OUT NOW!

Download My FREE Report
www.FormulaForMillionaires.com

Free Bonus #3

Formula For Millionaires
REPORT #3

Top 10 Money Myths ~ Outrageous Lies That *Keep Us Poor*

Have you fallen prey to believing
all the lies about money that keep you poor?
How do you know?
The truth makes you free.
Discover the truth about money…

FIND OUT NOW!

Download My FREE Report
www.FormulaForMillionaires.com

Free Bonus #4

Paul McCormick
Video & Audio

A wealth of tips
to help make YOU wealthy!

Informative • Entertaining • Invaluable

DOWNLOAD NOW!

They're all FREE at
www.FormulaForMillionaires.com

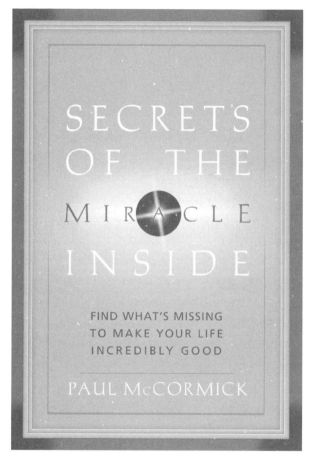

"This book will evoke the power of the soul and the spirit of
the power within you to reach for the stars
and live the life you desire.
You will be hearing lots about this book
and Paul McCormick.
Take the journey and change your life for Good."
~ Dr. Patricia A. Baccili, host of The Dr. Pat Show
Seattle, Washington

Additional books by Paul McCormick

Did you miss Paul's first book? Here's your chance to catch up on your reading. Purchase this book at any bookstore, or online (Amazon.com, etc.), or at www.TheSecretsInside.com

SECRETS of the
MIRACLE INSIDE

Find what's missing to make your life incredibly good.
You searched for answers, but didn't know
where to look or what to look for.
Perhaps you've lost hope that an answer exists.
An answer *does* exist. It remains a secret to most people.
This book shows where and how to find that secret
— the miracle that will transform your life forever.

YOU WILL DISCOVER:
HAPPINESS • FREEDOM • GOOD HEALTH
PURPOSE • PROSPERITY • PEACE

ISBN-13: 978-9794338-3-2
MIRACLE WRITERS, LLC PUBLISHING COMPANY

THESECRETSINSIDE.COM